Life, Culture and Education
on the Academic Plantation

Higher Ed

Questions about the Purpose(s) of Colleges & Universities

Norm Denzin, Josef Progler, Joe L. Kincheloe, Shirley R. Steinberg
General Editors

Vol. 2

PETER LANG
New York • Washington, D.C./Baltimore • Bern
Frankfurt am Main • Berlin • Brussels • Vienna • Oxford

Dierdre Glenn Paul

Life, Culture and Education on the Academic Plantation

Womanist Thought and Perspective

PETER LANG
New York • Washington, D.C./Baltimore • Bern
Frankfurt am Main • Berlin • Brussels • Vienna • Oxford

Library of Congress Cataloging-in-Publication Data

Paul, Dierdre Glenn.
Life, culture and education on the academic plantation: womanist
thought and perspective / Dierdre Glenn Paul.
p. cm. — (Higher ed; vol. 2)
Includes bibliographical references.
1. Afro-American women—Education (Higher). 2. Afro-American women
teachers. 3. Feminism and education—United States. 4. Discrimination
in higher education—United States. I. Title.
LC2781.5 .P28   378'.0082—dc21   00-056401
ISBN 0-8204-4562-2
ISSN 1523-9551

Die Deutsche Bibliothek-CIP-Einheitsaufnahme

Paul, Dierdre Glenn:
Life, culture and education on the academic plantation: womanist
thought and perspective / Dierdre Glenn Paul.
–New York; Washington, D.C./Baltimore; Bern;
Frankfurt am Main; Berlin; Brussels; Vienna; Oxford: Lang.
(Higher ed; Vol. 2)
ISBN 0-8204-4562-2

Cover design by Joni Holst

The paper in this book meets the guidelines for permanence and durability
of the Committee on Production Guidelines for Book Longevity
of the Council of Library Resources.

Printed in the United States of America

To Edward, Helen, Carolyn, Aliya, and Carol Brandon,
whose struggles have made it possible for me to write and
trangress, with freedom and without fear

Acknowledgments

I would like to thank Dean Nicholas Michelli and Linda Christian-Smith for their gentle guidance and strong belief in my work.

I would like to thank Tina Jacobowitz and Beverly Gordon for posing the tough questions and challenging me to think in new ways.

I thank Joe and Shirley for giving me a chance to be heard as well as Chris and Lisa for making the process a smooth one.

I thank Tamara and Ana Maria for reading drafts of this work and sharing their insights.

I truly wish to thank Marcia Schneider, Dr. Sharon Scherl, Eva, and Dr. Scherl's staff for offering me new lenses on the world.

Thank you Aunt Toni for being a model of strength during adversity.

I thank and acknowledge God each day.

Contents

Prologue

This collection of essays centers on my life experiences and identity as a Black woman living in a racially schizophrenic society, a single mother, a former public school teacher, a teacher educator, and an emerging intellectual. Through the processes of reflexivity and life history, I attempt to cohere the concentric spheres of race, gender, and class as they play themselves out in my daily living and multiple roles.

This book has a transformative agenda. In an ambitious fashion, I desire that most who read it be metamorphosed, whether that change be consequential and life-altering or manifest itself in modest ways. Transformation might take the form of more fully appreciating the world's complexity as a result of viewing it from a different set of lenses, becoming more cognizant of one's actions and the dispositions which prompt those actions, or committing to a more rigorous fight for social justice, across lines of positionality.

> The true focus of revolutionary change is never merely the oppressive situations which we seek to escape, but that piece of the oppressor which is planted deep within each of us, and which knows only the oppressor's tactics, the oppressor's relationships. Change means growth, and growth can be painful. But we sharpen self-definition by exposing the self in work and struggle together with those whom we define as different from ourselves, although sharing the same goals (Lorde 1984, 123).

While the themes of border transgression and plurality bind them all, the essays do not appear in any specific, predetermined order. In fact, if the reader were to approach this text by reading in a linear fashion, s/he might be perplexed by the seeming discontinuity that emerges. This book was not designed to be read in such a fashion. Instead, I would prefer that the reader broach these essays out of sequence and in the order of interest. Relatedly, the reader might notice some repetition in the varied essays. This authorial decision frees the reader to select at will.

It is my hope that this work is written in a fashion that displays the reflection and thought that went into its composition process and simultaneously proves accessible and reader-friendly to all who read it. While I hope that this book will serve to advance thought in academia and other educational arenas, I am saddened that it might not find its way into the hands of more people of color. A fact is that, in some instances, the language used will distance some of the very people it seeks to reach; it will shut them out. I am also prepared for criticism from academics who find the inclusion of Black English Vernacular and cursing disconcerting and unscholarly. I have attempted to ensure that the cursing is not gratuitous; that it presents the best word choice to convey the particular emotion or indignation that I am feeling or have felt.

In essence, "this is the oppressor's language, yet I need it to talk to you" (Rich as quoted in hooks 1990, 146). I have attempted to fuse the oppressor's language with that which is more accessible, even risqué. I have tried to transgress discursive borders.

I use this strategy in a deliberate fashion for the purpose of fucking up the power balance and creating disequilibrium. I desire for readers to be jarred by the language, forced to stop and consider the biases that affect the way in which words are used and evaluated.

The book is an amalgam of genres and writing styles. Some of the essays are more formal and academic than others; yet, privileging the personal unifies them all. The choice is a conscious one and based, once again, upon border transgression and the merging of boundary lines. This alternative writing approach might present an uneven read for some.

Chapter 1

Opposition and the Valuation of Difference

I usually define myself in oppositional terms—terms that directly contrast with the mainstream status quo. Opposition and the valuation of difference have been characterized as "that raw and powerful connection from which our personal power is forged" (Lorde 1984, 112).

In describing myself, the first adjectives that come to mind are "Black" and "female." I am a thirty-six year old, single mother, raising two children with the help of a strong support network that consists of my mother, grandmother, and sister. I am divorced.

I am a U.S. citizen; therefore, I position these essays within that context. While Blacks throughout the African Diaspora share similar experiences of oppression and domination and have developed shared coping mechanisms, representative of strength, resilience, and growth, my own experiences have occurred within the boundaries of the United States and that context shapes my thought.

These *positionalities* that I discuss, defined in this instance as race, gender, class, and "other aspects of our identities as markers of relational positions rather than essential qualities" (Maher and Tetreault 1993, 118; Alcoff 1988), are constructed and reconstructed through the process of social interaction. "Identity is socially produced, multiple, contradictory, and contingent. It is discursively constructed in real, local circumstances and often related to the ways in which powerful discourses are made available and circulate," (Apple and Oliver 1998, 124). Thus, society responds to me as a Black woman and my perceptions are shaped by my identity and interactions.

Though I am committed to improving the plight of us all from traditionally marginalized cultures, an injustice would be served and presumptuousness fostered if I attempted to fully represent all of our interests. I can only write knowledgeably about that which I have experienced . . . that which I have lived. As such, I write from the theoretical construct, cultural pluralism, advanced by W.E.B. DuBois. There are four tenets of cultural pluralism:

> 1) Each race has its own distinct and particular culture. 2) Different races can accept a common conception of justice and live together at peace in one nation-state. 3) Individuals must develop more and closer ties to the other members of their own race in order to preserve and enhance those cultural traits which mark it off from others. 4) . . . the cultural pluralist hastens to add that [s]he does not say that any particular culture is superior or inferior to any other, only that they are different, and that the members of each race must make a concerted effort to develop their own culture . . . because each race must present its culture as a gift to the other races (Boxill 1995, 236).

"Although I have tried to compensate for the limits of my particular social . . . history, I principally depend upon others to translate [and make applicable] across cultures" (Ruddick 1980, 347).

I am a Womanist teacher-scholar, specifically a teacher educator, who works in a university setting. The term "Womanist" was first introduced by Alice Walker (1983, xi). She defines it as: a Black feminist or feminist of color; committed to survival and wholeness of people, male and female; and wanting to know more and in greater depth than is considered 'good' for one.

I prefer the term "Womanist" to "Black Feminist" as "Womanist" was instituted by a Black woman to describe the experiences of Black women; but, I believe that the name is less significant than its purpose, which "encompasses theoretical interpretations of black women's reality by those who live it" (Collins 1990, 22). The term's genesis can be directly linked to Third Wave feminism. The Third Wave has characterized past feminisms as focusing predominantly on the experiences of White, middle-class women and universalizing those experiences as the experience of all women (Ideta and Cooper, 1999).

With past feminisms, other disturbing trends emerged regarding people of color. For one, a number of White feminists were co-conspirators with White men in the maintenance of hegemonic control and patriarchy, especially if their own desires were in danger of subjugation to Black interests. An example of this need for control is evidenced in the latter nineteenth-century struggle surrounding the issue of suffrage (Davis 1981; Gordon 1995). White feminists of the time strategically fought for their right to vote. In the process, however, they colluded with White men to impede Black men's acquisition of voting power and relegated Black women's concerns to the periphery (Davis 1981; Carby 1985; Gordon 1995; Marable 1996).

Also, many White feminists attempt to cast the burden of race in the same light as those of other oppressions, like gender, class, and sexual orientation. I beg to differ on this point. The pernicious and continuous onslaught against people of color in the United States makes it central to our history in a manner unlike any other oppression. In addition, people of color are recurrently affected by more than one oppression. For example, a number of our lives are impacted by both race and class. Women of color are often affected by the dynamics of race, class, and gender. Gays and lesbians of color are, far too frequently, subject to predatory attack and persecution that can center on race, class, gender, and sexual orientation.

I view myself as an emerging Black woman intellectual, in spite of the fact that the writer of a piece of hate mail I received stated that such a classification was "oxymoronic." I make the distinction between being an academic and an intellectual.

> An intellectual is not simply someone who trades in ideas . . . An intellectual is someone who trades in ideas by transgressing discursive borders, because he or she sees a need to do that. Secondly, an intellectual is somebody who trades in ideas in their vital bearing on a wider political culture (hooks 1991, 152).

When I use the identification *intellectual*, I use it as a means of stating that I am committed to a life of the mind, the development of a critical consciousness and political activism. I see literacy and education, not schooling necessarily, as means of emancipation and empowerment. As an educator, I am committed to the practice of a liberatory pedagogy (Gordon 1995; Lawrence 1995). Liberatory pedagogy emphasizes political praxis and approaches Black subject matter and that involving people of color in an empathic and culturally sensitive fashion. It displays commitment to social justice and community-building.

I consciously use the term "liberatory pedagogy" rather than "critical pedagogy" as a means of protesting the fact that many of the educational concepts and ideas espoused by the late Paulo Freire (in his conceptualization of education for critical consciousness) had been championed more than forty to fifty years earlier by W.E.B. DuBois and Carter G. Woodson, respectively, within the United States and regarding the education of Blacks primarily (Butchart 1994; Gordon 1994, 1995). While I do not begrudge nor minimize Freire's impact or influence, I consciously note the way in which White educators in the United States have been much more open to such ideas when they are proposed outside of the United States rather than deal with collective racism, its historic legacy, and the sustained negation of Black intellectuals and Black epistemology that have come to pass within the borders of the United States.

As a thinker and researcher, I rely on the conceptual bases of multicultural education, feminism, and critical race theory. Traditional feminist theory has proven problematic for me as a Black woman, as it has been for many people of color. Historically, feminist theory has served to bolster and replicate racism (Carby 1985). "Often feminist concerns are seen as a divisive, white importation that further fragments an already divided and embattled race, as trivial mind games unworthy of response while black people everywhere confront massive economic and social problems." (S.A. Williams 1990, 68).

Yet, Black women's concerns have often gone ignored and underestimated within the Black community in the name of race struggle. For instance, Black women were asked to support Black men in their quest for the vote during the late 1800s, knowing that we would not be granted that right simultaneously. Black women were asked to take back seats, within the ranks of the Black Panther Party, while Black men assumed the roles of leaders and thinkers. In the face of racism, contemporary Black women have frequently been asked to present a united front with Black men who don't support us (as evidenced by domestic violence rates within community and U.S. poverty rates for Black, female-headed households).

Personally, I cannot distinguish between the pain resulting from my status as Black and my status as female. It is just as painful to realize that attempts are being made to compromise my position or silence me because I am a woman, making business transactions or other consequential decisions, without a man by my side, as it is to realize that I am being targeted because I am Black.

I view traditional feminist theory as "water that contains some dirt. Because you are thirsty you are not too proud to extract the dirt and be nourished by the water" (hooks 1994, 50). Additionally, I must consider individual White women who have befriended me. In many instances, they have been most supportive of my development and expressed a steadfast belief in my capabilities. Black female intellectual Anna Julia Cooper challenged White women to divest from the bonds of racist patriarchy (Carby 1985). She determined that White women's re-education was one of her life's purposes. In this manner, she could gradually erode their propensity toward exclusionary practices and divisive words (Carby 1985). Though some have considered Cooper's mission naive, I take some credence in coalition-building, working with committed individuals, across lines of positionality, to affect systemic change.

Within the context of this volume, I desire to give primacy to a multidimensional and multifaceted discourse. I value the arts of storytelling and life history. In this sense:

> Story and narrative, whether personal or fictional, provide meaning and belonging in our lives. They attach us to others and to our own histories by providing a tapestry rich with threads of time, place, character, and even advice on what we might do with our lives. The story fabric offers us images, myths, and metaphors that are morally resonant and contribute both to our knowing and being known.

> The narrator too has a story, one that is embedded in his or her own culture, language, gender, beliefs, and life history. This embeddedness lies at the core of the teaching-learning experience (Witherell and Noddings as cited in Lewis 1993, 1)

Storytelling and life history serve as necessary ways through which to situate the voices of oppressed people as central to the telling of history and the construction of knowledge.

Within the context of this work, I use autobiography as a form of life history and a mode of reflexivity. Reflexivity, in this sense, refers to a consideration of the "intellectual autobiography" of researchers, since, according to Maynard (1993, 16), "the researcher is also a subject in her research and . . . her personal history is part of the process through which 'understanding' and 'conclusions' are reached.

The significance of personal or life history lies in the composition of "self-referential stories through which the author-narrator constructs the identity and point(s) of view of a unique individual historically situated in culture, time and place" (Chinn as quoted in Christian-Smith 1999, 45–46). The application of life history can serve as a powerful tool in the analysis of power dynamics and relational positions. I have adopted life history as a mode in which to make sense of the world and analyze the complex and paradoxical dynamics of race, class, gender, sexual orientation, and other positionalities.

Life history, through its use of both oral and written narrative, is a viable means of constructing epistemology, specifically Black epistemology, within the framework of this discussion. Black epistemology, as defined by Gordon (1990), is "the study or theory of the knowledge generated out of the [Black] existential condition" (90).

> Autobiographies of black women, each of which is necessarily personal and unique, constitute a running commentary on the collective experience of black women in the United States. . . . Their common denominator . . . derives not from the

general categories of race or sex, but from the historical experience of being black and female in a specific society at a specific moment and over succeeding generations. Black women's autobiographies resist reduction to either political or critical pieties and resist even more firmly reduction to mindless empiricism (Fox-Genovese, 1990, 178–179).

The life stories of Black women evoke an awareness of the "convergence of racism, sexism, and class antagonism [that] marks the Third World woman's peculiar position in discourse . . . and calls into question the truth value of any unitary or dualistic apprehension of the world" Wallace 1990, 65).

Traditionally, autobiographical accounting recorded by people of color, especially women, has been evaluated more stringently, in respect to issues of veracity and memory (Etter-Lewis 1993). For many of us, there has been and remains no incentive to lie. Yet, it is my belief that our accounts are judged in this fashion because they present harsh truths that society would rather ignore and discredit. As it has historically dealt with prophets, society chooses to discount the message by compromising the messenger.

From the time of the slave narrative, many Black women's voices have been "silenced" and muted by the harsh double standard that has been employed in the evaluation of Black female autobiography (Etter-Lewis 1993).

Ultimately, this Black woman will not be silenced. "From the perspective of dominance, a woman of color who insists on functioning as a speaking (writing) subject threatens the status of Truth itself" (Wallace 1990, 65).

The purpose of this collection of autobiographical essays is not unlike that of tagging. Tagging, an aspect of hip hop culture—a culture of which I am intimate and familiar—describes an urban, folk art form that developed into graffiti. Artists who tag do it as a way of validating their existences. It is a means of establishing that their lives, thoughts, and art mean something. Though it frequently offends middle-class sensibilities, it is created to be bold, strident, and provocative.

This book is my tag. As it is autobiographical in nature, it may be considered an imprecise recording of events shaped through a singular set of lenses and perceptions. My memories of certain occurrences will not necessarily be those of others, nor should they be.

Others will focus on supposed contradictions in thought. Yet, mere everyday living is a contradiction. We grow, we change, we rethink our positions. I make no claims of neutrality or objectivity. My work is, decidedly, political and subjective.

In the process of revelation, it is a given that some information disclosed will be intensely personal. I have made a conscious decision to reveal only that which I deem as helpful, attempting to stay clear of that which is merely prurient. Additionally, I realize that there will be some information that family, friends, and colleagues might find painful. Yet, that remains a risk run in the process of autobiographical accounting.

Upon reading this collection, there will be those who deduce that I am "too idealistic, too reductive, too sophomoric, too angry" (Dilks 1998, 161). In a response to an earlier version of the second essay appearing in this volume (originally published in Kathleen Dixon's edited collection *Outbursts in Academe: Multiculturalism and Other Sources of Conflict*), scholar Stephen Dilks thoughtfully cautions against such efforts to invalidate. He states:

> If academe is to continue its contributions to the development of a truly democratic social structure, it needs to figure out how to listen to those whose very presence reveals institutionally sanctioned behaviors and actions to be antiegalitarian, contradictory, hypocritical, deceitful, wrong. If education is to remain central to our institutional practices, we need to figure out how to read an essay like Paul's without resorting to clichés about diplomacy, maturity and decorum (161).

I am in no way deterred by contentions about my intellect or maturity. After all, aren't these claims reflective of the age-old struggle that intellectuals who are women and/or people of color face? Far too frequently, our work is dismissed as not warranting serious thought. We are deemed "angry," "hypersensitive," or "hysterical." All this makes perfect sense when one reflects on historical attempts to infantilize and negate our thought (Morton 1991; Steinem 1993).

Through *Life, Culture, Education on the Academic Plantation: Womanist Thought and Perspective*, I hope to validate not only my own experiences and stories, but those of other women scholars and people of color who struggle *each day* to have their voices heard rather than muted; fight for their rightful places within the academy and contest prevailing thought on knowledge construction and for whom that knowledge should be of benefit. If life within the academy has *ever* made you feel "crazy, marginalized, a fringe person or out of touch," this book is written for you as a vehicle of affirmation (Nelson 1993, 244).

It is my anticipation that this book will proclaim that there is one more of "us" out there contesting privilege and attempting to make the academy live up to its rhetoric of inclusion, democracy, and liberal thought. Yet, more significantly, the declaration must be made that *we are here to stay*. We are not going anywhere. In her book *Sex, Lies, and Stereotypes:*

Perspectives of a Mad Economist (1994, 216), author Julianne Malveaux relates:

> If you don't like it here, why don't you leave? People ask me that all the time, reminding me that there is more liberty here than in some totalitarian country. They may have a point, but I'm not going anywhere—my ancestors built this country as much as anyone else's did, even though they didn't get paid for it. I don't believe in the adage love it or leave it. I think the words are improve it or lose it.

Malveaux's words resonate within me. "Not to complain about real inequities and real sources of misery in even the most powerful institutions seems only to kowtow to power rather than participate in a meaningful and great-souled manner" (P.J. Williams 1991, 94).

The academy will have to improve. Through the efforts of many, the academy will be forced to make room for us. As Frederick Douglass most eloquently stated, "power concedes nothing without demand." If enough of us start making the demand, change is bound to occur.

Chapter 2

Young, Black, and Female in Academe

Introduction

Many who critique institutions do so from outside of establishment walls. They have either left the institution or plan to leave prior to the critique's publication. I do not condemn such critics because critique is both personally and professionally risky. As a result of speaking out, one's livelihood might be jeopardized and chances for future success potentially minimized.

In my estimation, however, transformation can best be achieved by those who work from within to effect it. This conviction has created an undeniable tension in respect to this essay's composition. In writing and revising, speaking truth and maintaining credibility have remained primary in importance. Concurrently, I must situate the account in a fashion that does not hinder White allies in their continuing efforts to diversify the faculty nor thwart their attempts to enhance conditions in which plurality might thrive. I must acknowledge my Dean's battles to hire and retain faculty of color and appreciate his administration's labors to address issues of democracy and diversity. Similarly, I recognize the efforts of campus-based, White faculty who have actively sought to support my scholarship through grant awards, tenure, and promotion. These constituencies have served as stable sources of support and encouraged me in the writing of this book (even after reading this chapter), though they also cautioned me to consider the potential hindrance posed if other people of color read the work and attributed the racism described as particular to Montclair State University or the College of Education and Human Services (CEHS).

Additionally, I have deliberated on the status of other, campus-based people of color, as well as myself, as we have and continue to make gains in power. The advances enable us to open doors for others of us from traditionally marginalized cultures and accelerate the change process, so that the academy honors its expressed commitment to democracy, inclusion, and liberal thought. I do not wish for my actions to be perceived as an impediment to that progress.

Candidly, I play the game to the extent that it buys me the freedom to take risks and improve academic life for people of color and women. For me, playing the game does not necessarily mean making myself available to mentor students of color or trying to secure an administrative position, though such efforts are certainly worthwhile. In the tradition of many scholars of color who came before me and whose struggles have earned me a place within academy walls, I am concerned with the production of exemplary scholarship, broadening the range of epistemological models deemed acceptable within academic circles, further advancing the "conceptualization of knowledge as constructed, contested, incessantly perspectival and polyphonic" (Lather 1986, 13) and privileging Black knowledge construction processes as different and equivalently consequential rather than deficient.

It is equally important to state that, even with such commitment as demonstrated by the CEHS Dean, his administration, some White faculty and a cadre of faculty of color, racism continues to make some strides. Within the context of this essay, I chronicle occurrences on this particular campus. *I do not assert that such problems are specific to it.* My intent is *not* to single out either the CEHS or Montclair. Instead, I wish to state, emphatically, that the acts and sentiments described are endemic to the academy generally, as they are embedded in the societal infrastructure. My experiences mirror those of other scholars from traditionally marginalized cultures, within the context of this discussion Black women intellectuals, on predominantly White campuses throughout the United States.

Unfortunately, some of the stories presented have been more degrading and malevolent than those that I present. For instance, I reflect on Angela Davis's discussions of her firing (centered on her politics) from the University of California in Los Angeles. I ponder the experience of Ruth Farmer, as related in *Spirit, Space and Survival: African American Women in (White) Academe* (James and Farmer, 1993), whose position at Barnard College was mysteriously eliminated or lost in "restructuring" as a reward for her efforts to diversify the College's Center for Research on Women (3).

One is led to question the way in which faculty of color are expected to survive within climates like those described by anthropologist Leith Mullings (1997). Mullings presents instances in which the painted word "nigger" appeared near her Columbia University office door and an enigmatic fire was set (in her office) that consumed two years of lecture notes.

Finally, I *feel* the experiences legal scholar Patricia Williams (1991) recounts during which fellow law professors deem her scholarship as "emotional stuff," student evaluation forms define her as "condescending, earthy, approachable and arrogant" and one student characterizes Professor Williams's braids as being wrapped around her "great bald dome of a skull." I imagine Williams's face as a white male student in one of her seminars stood before his classmates and read a Rudyard Kipling poem to her. The poem compared the relative lustiness of white, brown, yellow, and 'nigger' women. The incident was recorded in her essay "*Talking About Race, Talking about Gender, Talking About How We Talk*" (1996).

There are countless other descriptions of such injustices, reported in the forms of personal anecdote (related orally) and varied writings. As I hear and read them, my commitment becomes more deeply entrenched that such experiences, including my own, must become obsolete. With these thoughts expressed, I present my story . . . a story that is written as much for those who have left academia, voluntarily or without choice, as for those who stay and fight from within.

My Story

Some moments are indelible in memory. For me, such an occasion was my 1993 job interview at a state university located in a Northeastern suburb. I was impressed with the campus' pastoral beauty, including the flowering blossoms and picturesque buildings I entered. I still recall the warm welcome of the interview team, including CEHS faculty and the dean. After the interview, I felt enthusiastic, and looked forward to the possibility that I would find, on that attractive campus and within the friendly department, my niche in academe. I had just completed my doctoral work at Teachers College; only the writing and defense of the dissertation remained. My hopes were high of landing a job right out of school. Becoming a professor was a long-held dream.

When the official offer arrived, euphoria swept over me. My family, my then-fiancé and I celebrated my entry into the "big time." As we say in the Bronx, "My shit was tight." But the Bronx was a very different place . . . quite different from this new space. In fact, I didn't realize the depth of the difference at that time. I had been a resident of the Bronx for twenty-two years and, after completing my undergraduate studies, I taught there as well.

Keepin' It Real: Classrooms in the Bronx

I had six years of experience in an intermediate school and a year-long position as an elementary school, Communication Arts teacher trainer. My self-defined mission in the predominantly Black and Latino, Bronx-based classrooms in which I taught was to provide my students with the rules of access (as defined by the dominant culture). I am defining "access" as the knowledge and skills needed for class mobility, increased earning potential, and opportunity. I wished to enable my students to use those rules for their own benefit, as well as that of their communities. Determining an educational plan that would enhance their facility with standard English, providing them with greater access to society, and countering the social ills they routinely encountered were of utmost importance to me.

My concern was engendered as a result of growing up and attending school in the same community as my students, then receiving the opportunity to attend an exclusive boarding school in Pittsfield, Massachusetts. The experience permitted me to see the disparity between education (in the United States) for the White elite compared with education for the working class and/or poor people of color. Differences were evident in everything from the educational materials used to the instructional format.

As a teacher returning to the Bronx classroom, I quickly realized that without the ability to read and understand the power inherent in the written word, a number of my students (as happened to many of my public school classmates) would be relegated to existences in which drugs, prison, dropping out, and poverty played inevitable roles.

Some of my intermediate school students were aliterate. They could read, meaning they could both decode and comprehend. Yet, reading proved to be a bore, especially when there was Nintendo, Sega Genesis, television, rap, Arnold Schwarzenegger, and Jean Claude Van Damme videotapes to be explored.

Other students hated reading because it was a source of both difficulty and embarrassment. In their minds, it had caused other students to laugh at them during those famed round-robin reading sessions. It had caused teachers to sacchrinely smile and say "That was nice reading" when the snickers in the back of the classroom clearly indicated that it was a far cry from "nice." It had also caused teachers to yell, "Can't you read?" Sometimes I ponder on what would have happened if a student had yelled back at that instant, "What the fuck is wrong with you . . . can't you teach me to read?" Of course, I know the answer to that. But, it remains an entertaining thought, nonetheless.

In the spirit of fairness, however, I must acknowledge that these students' problems with literacy did not evolve solely from formalized educational experiences. Some students' problems resulted from a disposition (expressed in their homes) that formal education was a lower priority than survival. This attitude could be gleaned from comments made by both parents and children in this community. For example, some parents shared that, as per the dictates of their socioeconomic reality, work was and would remain the priority. Everything else, including their children's academic performance, was of secondary importance. I clearly understood that mere survival was an everyday struggle for such families living in the most "advanced" nation in the modern world . . . an "advanced" nation in which approximately one in five children under the age of eighteen lives in poverty (Children's Defense Fund 1996).

A potential consequence of such an unjust battle is children who cannot read. Children from backgrounds in which school is given little merit do not exhibit the same degree of literacy as children from school-oriented households (Heath 1983).

Other parents harbored antipathetic feelings about the school culture as a result of their own experiences and/or antagonistic and patronizing encounters with school administrators regarding their children. In many ways, these parents were justifiably rebelling against the school culture as the dominant culture and the implications surrounding that premise. As alluded to and/or discussed by Delpit (1988), Edelsky and Harman (1991), and Willis (1995), these parents from traditionally marginalized cultures were painfully aware that the school culture was unresponsive and unable to cope with the needs of their children as evidenced by the curriculum addressed, discipline used, and educational materials selected. Unfortunately, school systems as hegemonic entities don't respond well to the children of dissidents.

Although my goals for my students were clearly defined, the pedagogical strategies I would potentially employ were not. In a number of instances, teaching was trial and error. I was unaware of the kind of theory that would support my beliefs or shape my pedagogical practice. Like most teachers of color, I commenced teaching through an alternate certification route. There simply were not enough teachers to meet the demands of a growing New York City student population, Thus, at twenty-one years of age, with a degree in English/journalism and without the benefit of an education course—or even one focusing upon literacy development or children's/adolescent literature—I was required to teach the children in my charge.

The task was daunting at first; but, it became easier. As time elapsed, teaching even became exciting and liberating. I grew to value the experiential, sending the message that reading and writing were fun and should result in social action. I desired that communication arts become relevant to students' lives and I attempted to ensure that class activities and projects reflected my values.

For example, my sixth and seventh grade students and I discussed social responsibility. The discussion emerged as a result of their interest in a book that I was reading entitled *Diet for New America* (Robbins 1987) and from which I shared excerpts with them. Subsequently, both groups determined (of their own volition) that they weren't as socially responsible as they desired.

As a result of our dialogue, the sixth graders organized a schoolwide, canned goods drive. They publicized the event, collected the cans, contacted a community-based organization that would handle subsequent distribution, and clearly defined their expectations of me. By all accounts, their project was a success. Most significantly, however, they left my classroom with the firm understanding that their actions had a positive impact upon society. This message directly contrasted with the one they routinely received from local, televised newscasts regarding their communities and themselves as reflections of those communities.

My seventh graders were concerned about the environment. They decided to target McDonald's restaurants. A number of them decided to boycott until the chain stopped using Styrofoam cups and containers. Others decided that, while they could not forego McDonald's hamburgers, they could remain in solidarity with their classmates by requesting that their Big Macs be wrapped in paper. The seventh graders also composed and circulated petitions and held a schoolwide rally on the environment. Many teachers and students nationally have been involved in similar efforts regarding McDonald's. Yet, that fact does not minimize the importance of my class's efforts nor negate the lesson that there is power in protest.

In another instance, students explored the question, "What is poetry?" In my experience, many students appeared to bring limited knowledge of the topic to discussions and understood only a narrow scope of the genre, such as a few traditional poets like Shakespeare and Edgar Allan Poe. Students seemed to associate poetry with boredom and antiquity. Through exposure to and discussion of nontraditional poets and definitions of poetry, I was able to assist them in establishing a broader conceptualization. They were encouraged to collaboratively define poetry in cooperative learning groups, as well as define it through probing the "poetry" in various media forms, like art, song, rap, greeting cards, motion, dance, and nursery rhymes.

I was most excited by their enthusiasm over the discovery that rap music, an aspect of urban culture with which many of them were familiar, was a valid poetic form, that included rhyme, meter, figurative language, and significant theme. Legitimately, rap could be classified as poetry because "regardless of a poet's culture, that poet uses rhythm, imagery, typography, grammar, and syntax as the medium of the poem" (Purves 1993, 358).

There were instances when I witnessed personal change of great consequence in individual students; for example, one of my students, who was most concerned with following the school rules and pleasing others, developed her own voice during one of our classes. After we had read a contemporary fiction book, entitled *Going Home* (Mohr 1986) and featuring a Latina heroine, this young woman courageously stated that she was tired of hearing everyone else's story, those of Blacks and Whites. She desired to hear more Latina/o stories. Soon after, she entered a piece in a writing contest on her experiences as a Latina, won, and was published in a local newspaper.

As I became more proficient at teaching, children (even some of the most hardened) laughed and smiled in my classroom on a regular basis. I was often told by the children, their parents, and colleagues that the children loved both my class and me. Parents and colleagues were overwhelmingly supportive of my efforts, even those attempts that were unconventional. In many instances, we shared similar concerns and hopes. A bond of trust had been secured.

I was passionate in my work, and I was confident about my burgeoning approach to education and literacy. My experiences evoked the erotic within. In this sense, "erotic" is defined as:

> an assertion of the life-force of women; of that creative energy empowered, the knowledge and use of which we are now reclaiming in our language, our history, our dancing, our loving, our work, our lives (Lorde 1984, 55).

Simultaneously, I began taking education courses. Soon after, I commenced my full-time doctoral studies in evening classes while continuing to teach full-time during the day. In the process, I discovered theory focusing upon multicultural education that strongly supported my practice.

Cross Questions and Crooked Answers: Students at the State University

I had been deeply affected by my classroom experiences, especially the context in which I taught, involving Black and Latino, working class and poor families. After my doctoral studies, I arrived on the university campus with a publicly acknowledged commitment to multicultural education.

But, I found myself looking into a vast sea of primarily White female faces in my education courses and seeing (in a number of them) disdain for and a lack of comprehension of both the concepts I was addressing and of me. In spite of the college's mission and commitment to innovative pedagogical practice, many of my students would place their notebooks neatly on the desk (at the start of each class) and wait for me to lecture. My questions were met with silence. Attempts to initiate dialogic exchange concerning the political and social dynamics of literacy instruction were often perceived as "a waste of time" or opportunities to attack liberal, progressive ideas.

Class assignments had to be reviewed (ad nauseum) until each minute detail was explained. This particular set of students, who were mostly early childhood majors, complained, "We won't be able to teach kids to read after this course." They seemed to disregard, totally, the fact that the course I taught was an introductory overview to the field of early literacy development.

Their scorn and lack of comprehension also was revealed in the student evaluations I received. For example, students wrote:

> I strongly feel that most of her information is good but not appropriate for this class. Yes, multiculturalism can be tied to reading and literature, however, Mrs. Glenn has spent sooo much and too much time on this subject alone . . . She comes across as very prejudice [sic] and is very offensive.

> The instructor was apparently a well-read person . . . I felt her focus on African American content was distracting and quite offensive.

> Stop using racism as a drive for all lessons, readings, videos, and most class discussions.

> Often goes off on tangents.

I felt a similar contempt for them; many of whom, in my estimation, suffered from "Good White Girl Syndrome," as a White, female colleague termed it. In fairness to this group of students and to mitigate the plausible perception that I have flippantly described the students' concerns, this syndrome is explicated in *Women's Ways of Knowing: The Development of Self, Voice, and Mind* (Belenky et al. 1986). The authors characterize the "good girl" as a young woman who has been

> rewarded for her quiet predictability, her competent though perhaps unimaginative work, and her obedience and conformity. This kind of 'good girl' when confronted with diversity and what seems to be the arbitrariness of truth and values, suddenly begins to feel that her world is unanchored (65).

I quickly tired of what I perceived as their intellectual cowardice. I had come to appreciate the profession of teaching for its ability to transform and emancipate. Yet, it appeared as if a number of my students were prepared to enter teaching as a diversion . . . until the right man came along. A lot of their pre-class and post-class talk seemed to center upon "my boyfriend" or ways in which to get a boyfriend to propose.

Surprisingly, complaints were not solely the province of my White students. It soon became evident that some of my students of color had labeled me a "sellout" to use the lingo of the city. In their eyes, I had forgotten where I came from and displayed little allegiance. To them, I was deemed unwilling to "keep it real." I recall most vividly the comment of an older Black female student (who had not completed assignments in a satisfactory manner, habitually arrived to class late, and slept through classes from time to time). She said, " I thought a Black professor would try a little harder to understand. I was wrong. When I teach, I will try to understand my Black students." In a typically bombastic fashion, my response was something to the effect of, "Don't give me that. You won't be helping. Mediocrity is expected by the dominant culture. Black children should be made to understand *that*, and thus, understand the need for excellence in all of their endeavors."

In another instance, a Latino male (who had a number of difficulties with spoken and written language) became so angry after a discussion regarding his end-term grade that he stormed out of my office saying, "It's no use talking to you." He previously shared with me his negative educational experiences, resulting from his lack of facility with English and his previous teachers' lack of cultural understanding. As he left my office after that heated exchange, I was profoundly saddened. I knew that I would be added to his list of negative experiences. But, on both occasions with the two students of color, I also knew that I was obligated, as a teacher-educator, to the children that they would go on to teach.

There was a major difference, however, between my discontented students of color and those who were White. The White female students were much more apt to challenge my authority. Without hesitation, they went to more established, older, White professors to discuss secretly my "progressive, radical beliefs," my "racism," "the difficult assignments" I gave, and my "lofty" academic standards. I was also "reported" because I was "advocating homosexuality" by asking students to critique the appropriateness of children's books focusing on gay and lesbian parents that had sparked controversy when they were introduced as part of New York City's Rainbow Curriculum.

A common student complaint was, "I just don't know what she wants. Why can't she just tell me what she wants and I'll give it to her!" While they claimed that they did not know what I wanted, I believed that I clearly knew what they wanted—boring, uninspired teaching. My instructional decision making was affected directly by the uncertainty and discomfort that I saw in their eyes. I had been told that many of them had never had a professor or teacher of color during their academic careers. Once during class, a student freely shared, with a smile, her pleasure of having made my acquaintance. She said, possibly without realizing that the comment could be pejorative, "Usually when I look at the news, I say, 'Oh, the Black people are acting up again.' You've helped me to see that there is diversity, all Black people don't act that way."

There were other White students who chose to include me among the ranks of "honorary Whites" like Oprah Winfrey and Michael Jordan. They also asked me for my opinion on supposed "renegade" Blacks like Louis Farrakhan or the late Khalid Muhammad. Legal scholar Derrick Bell (1992) describes this phenomenon as Whites seeking to validate their own interpretations and perceptions on renegade people of color by attempting to find another person of color who will criticize the rebel. If the critic does condemn, s/he gains in prestige and status for the authentication of White fear. Students were sometimes taken aback as I familiarized them with this phenomenon as a response to their questions.

I was frequently told that I was different from other Blacks. Some of the most prominent and remembered descriptors in this distinction by students and colleagues alike were "articulate" and "bright." For me, the most stinging was "articulate" because the assumption seemed to be that Blacks were not. I also recall being told by a White male student of the way in which I had pulled myself up "out of the ghetto" and become a productive member of society. This statement was made in front of my class on the first day of the semester. I responded, in front of the class, saying quite clearly and directly that the statement was "racist."

Such comments were often made without the benefit of much biographical information regarding my identity. I was always cognizant of students' attempts to place me into neat, stereotypical categories. Unfortunately, similarly convoluted attempts were made by university colleagues, White and Black.

Faculty and Me, A Woman Without a Country

On a regular basis, veteran colleagues would dismiss my concerns about students and assure me that student complaints were commonplace for new professors, regardless of race, creed, or color. Possibly such assurances would have been more credible if these colleagues had shared similar experiences, recounting their own narratives of novitiate in academe. They did not.

Additionally, these colleagues held entire conversations about my "arrogance" and "difficulty" in stairwells and other inappropriate venues, during which students and I both overheard. To the present day, I am certain that these colleagues were unaware that I heard them. I was cautioned that I made people "uptight." I didn't make small talk or share anecdotes. It was also stated that there wasn't a comfortable "fit" between my department members and myself; thus, there was explicit speculation that they would attempt to deny me tenure.

There were also times during which friends related instances in which they had been asked for help in dealing with my "anger" or explaining my idiosyncrasies. I was disgusted because it seemed very much like the way in which one might ask an "expert" about the habits of an exotic primitive.

While I choose against totally rejecting their claims, I believe that many of their comments and dismissals reflected my White colleagues' desire to focus on similarity, universality, and racelessness as opposed to acknowledging that the interpretations, perspectives, and worldviews of people from traditionally marginalized cultures might be quite different from their own, and equally valid. In this manner, any failing was purely personal and, as one colleague told me, "my problem." By dealing with the dilemma in this fashion, many of my coworkers could relinquish their own culpability for the situation at hand. Concomitantly, however, it became easier for them to deny my humanity as well.

Inherent in this discussion is the fact that my colleagues were often unable to acknowledge their White privilege and the undeniable advantage it provided them. Morrison (1992, 9–10) eloquently explains this occurrence by stating, "the habit of ignoring race is understood to be a graceful, even generous, liberal gesture. To notice is to recognize an already discredited difference." She further states that "the world does not become unracialized by assertion. The act of enforcing racelessness . . . is itself a racial act" (46).

An unfortunate result of my perceptions regarding colleagues' lack of acknowledgment of and respect for my difference was self-imposed isolation. In an effort to preserve my independence and dignity, I stopped consulting with a number of co-workers. I began to reject offers to collaborate, even though there were a few I maintained. One of them was my participation in a Women's Studies book discussion group. If memory serves, I was the only woman of color in the group who attended regularly. The others were White. I loved the books we read, the challenging debate, and the fresh perceptions with which I walked away. I met a number of women whom I admired. They seemed truly interested in listening, learning, and guiding the development of a young scholar.

With greater regularity, I refrained from asking other professors for suggestions on teaching strategies or instructional materials because a schism had developed and solidified. Instead, I read a great deal and incorporated my new learnings into my pedagogical repertoire.

My feelings of isolation intensified as I recognized the "discursive violence" (Kellor, 1999) employed by a number of colleagues, Black and White. Discourse was rife with "element{s} of one-upmanship" (Tannen, 1990, 24). To me, they attempted to clearly establish that I was in the subordinate position and others were in a "superordinate" one.

There were a number of times when I responded passively. For instance, during a meeting to determine the suitability of proposed doctoral courses, a discussion of ethnocentricism and its implications arose among committee members. Quite specifically, I broached the fact that the way in which a statement was worded seemed to imply that there was an uncontested, singular American educational philosophy which was Eurocentered and that the U.S. system was better than those within the global community. I assume that my thoughts were so incoherent and unintelligible that one man needed translation in several different forms. It seems odd to me that he clearly understood my two translators. For the sake of fairness, I must also state that the man to whom I allude did come to my office later that day to invite further discussion so that we could determine the point at which we disagreed.

Though not the case in this instance, my words routinely gain validity only after a White powerbroker or "interpreter" gives them credence. Unfortunately, that credence can sometimes come in the form of co-opting my points and making them theirs.

It is sad to say, but I have become accustomed to White colleagues' words and actions that suggest, "Why do we let these people in here?" The negation of my thought as a Black woman in such settings is commonplace for me. After all, covert racism works in this fashion. Reyes and Halcon (1996), identify *covert racism* as "the most pervasive form of racism in higher education. Because of its elusive nature . . . [it] is ignored by those who have never experienced it, and denied by those who contribute to it" (92). The ongoing and pervasive racism with which scholars of color must contend on a daily basis and which excludes them from complete and consequential participation in the academy translates into the *academic colonialism* described by Reyes and Halcon (1996) and Arce (1978).

> The fact that scholarly racism is subtle, rather than blatant, and institutional, rather than individual, makes it all the more an insidiously oppressive and effective dimension of the ideological apparatus that justifies and supports patterns of racist thought and behavior in the public domain and in the socioeconomic macrostructure (Smitherman 1988, 145).

In another instance with the same committee, I had used the word "change agentry" in a piece of writing that had to be revised three times prior to being deemed acceptable. After this process, it was determined that the piece would not be used at all. I was told that "change agentry" wasn't a word, even though I had seen it in a number of my readings. Other committee members chuckled over my faux pas. I smiled to hide my humiliation.

I was, ultimately, asked to substitute the phrase "change agency." I did. At a later point, however, a White female administrator used the term "change agentry" in a course outline reviewed by the group. She was asked about it and merely stated that it was in the "literature" without any specific attribution. There was no further challenge, there was no laughter. In both instances, I simply chose not to fight. In fact, after the meeting, one of my "translators" even asked me about my passivity. In more instances than not, I have fought fire with fire and gone into battle-mode.

During many of these allegedly academic debates, Whites characterize their strident interrogation and quixotic nitpicking as an engagement in intellectual debate and rigor. *It is not.* It is combative, denigrating, and elitist. Further, I distinguish between disagreement and interrogation. I am not personally threatened when someone respectfully disagrees with a point I make (as long as I have been *heard*). During interrogation, however, I am angered by the tone of condescension that frequently accompanies requests for clarification and elaboration when posed by Whites to people of color.

In a number of instances (such as the meetings discussed), I have felt tears attempting to rise. I maintained an appearance of detachment and being steely-eyed. I willed myself not to cry. For the most part, I will not cry in the presence of others, though I have often felt like it, especially on this campus, as attacks of all sorts have come without cessation. With assaults coming from every direction and outbursts flying, I increasingly felt the need to insulate myself with an ever-thickening wall of hostility, and an assertive and prepossessing style.

While there have been many instances in which Black male professors have been exceptionally kind and loving to me, there have also been occasions when I have addressed a Black male colleague's condescension and paternalism. For instance, during a faculty development program designed to assist in the retention of untenured professors, I noticed that our White male facilitator seemed to defer to a Black male colleague (who also happened to be a novice professor). It appeared as if my fellow novice was being touted as the authority on the position of untenured professors within this small group. I was especially sensitive to this distinction because my Black male colleague was the only other male present. The other participants were female.

During the course of the program, my awareness of this situation heightened, as well as my perception that this male colleague would interrupt as I spoke and attempt to solve problems (in an overly simplistic manner), when I merely needed a listening ear. His behavior seemed sanctioned by the group. So, one day, as my female colleagues sat silently or appeared conciliatory, I lit into him with a vengeance. I told him that I resented his implications that his thoughts were more valuable than mine and I addressed the fact that his patriarchal, myopic approach to problem solving did not work for all participants, as he had obviously assumed.

Needless to say, my behavior was not well received by some Black co-workers. An established Black, female professor called me aside to caution against what she termed "my obsessive-compulsive tendencies" and the need to tone down my responses. While I found her words objectionable, I felt there was little malice in her message. I believe that she sincerely viewed me as young, confused, and needing direction. In her mind, my most prominent concerns should have been to retain my position, gain political allies on campus, and ardently support other Black faculty.

For me, however, the most significant concerns have been to retain my integrity and individuality at any cost.

I recognized that I was entering combat . . . a battle to maintain my identity, define myself as a scholar *on my own terms*, and survive this experience emotionally intact in the face of adversity.

Generally, I felt that faculty attempts to reinforce the power structure, in their exchanges with me, were based on my race and/or gender. I also believe that the problematic nature of the situation was often exacerbated by my youth, assertiveness, and personal style. Additionally, the fact that I desired to effect change after being on campus for a short while did not help, either.

For example, more problems arose when I suggested that my department explore the possibility of adding a course to its offerings that focused on multicultural issues as they relate to pedagogy. The suggestion came within a month of my arrival on campus and from a twenty-eight year old. My proposal was largely based on my campus-related experiences with students. While I freely admit that I did not understand the politics of adding courses or academic turf battles, I was motivated by a desire to help. From my perspective, the suggestion was not an attempt to criticize the existing program. It was an attempt to improve upon it. A number of department members, however, viewed the recommendation as a bold affront. I expeditiously received the message that I had not yet "earned" the right to suggest changes. Granted, I understood their position that one should spend a certain amount of time within a structure before determining to change it (in any way). Yet, when does one earn the right to suggest changes? Is not this sense of earned privilege another means by which to reinforce the hierarchical nature of academe that so many within express the desire to change? Do not such attempts to maintain power structures prohibit the development of community within academe and respective departments?

In retrospect, I am sure that many colleagues were taken aback by my "arrogance" and desire to do things "my way." After all, it probably seemed that I wasn't happy even after they had been gracious enough to let me into "the club" (Etter-Lewis 1993). Friends have also told me that when White folk look at a 5'2" Black woman, wearing little glasses, conservatively dressed, and soft-spoken, they are not at all prepared for "who you really are." Yet, in my estimation and that of some others, I bring a new energy to academe, a definite perspective, an expanded interpretation of my field, and a distinctive approach to scholarship.

Revelations . . . How I Got My Groove Back

One Sunday morning, I saw novelist Terry McMillan discuss her book *How Stella Got Her Groove Back*. When asked to explain the title's genesis, she stated that, like the protagonist, she had temporarily lost her way in life. The deaths of her mother and best friend precipitated her disconsolation and confusion. Then, like Stella, McMillan went to Jamaica and experienced a spiritual and emotional renewal. She had once again taken control of her life. As I listened, I thought about the suitability of McMillan's title in relation to my own life. I also have taken control of my life once again.

In my Bronx classroom, I had developed a level of comfort with students and parents that made teaching an invigorating experience. I often left my classroom energized by the depth of my young students' responses. I also appreciated the support I received from colleagues of all races and ethnicities. The students, their parents, my colleagues, and I were in accord.

My positive experiences in the Bronx were predicated upon my conscious desire to teach Black and Latino youngsters in an urban center. I felt and continue to feel a deep sense of commitment to and concern for the plight of oppressed people. Such commitment has been expressed by Mary Church Terrell, W.E.B. DuBois, Ida Wells Barnett, Anna Julia Cooper, Maria Stewart, Carter G. Woodson, and continues to concern scholars of color globally (Banks, 1992). But, it seems the expression of such concern and commitment within the boundaries of my new arena (a predominantly White, suburban campus) was considered "racist" by a number of White students and colleagues. Many of my students had been trained to believe that the act of teaching was apolitical. It clearly is not. According to Pagano (as cited in Lewis 1999, 59):

> all teaching is political, even teaching which disclaims its politics. . . . For to teach is to bring others to look at things in new ways, to reorient them to the horizon of their world. That we are changed in the process of education is no mere accident. We teachers want to change our students. And we are certain that change is for the better.

My students, seemingly, believed that education was treating all students equally rather than equitably, as well as keeping one's politics out of the classroom. It might be more accurate to state that these were their expectations of me. *Their* feelings and politics were revealed consistently, as was their deference to other professors.

In my estimation, my students' expectations were retrograde and manifestations of their White privilege. The term *apolitical teaching* seemed a contradiction of monumental proportion. The politics of education are inherent in decisions ranging from curriculum design to those that are pedagogical in nature, especially as they continually disadvantage people of color and women.

In spite of our ideological differences, I was most indignant about the power I felt this new set of students wielded, mainly in overly subjective student evaluation forms that were masqueraded as "objective" measures (McCall 1999) and the way in which that power affected my pedagogical decision making. A number of feminist scholars cite similar examples of students using evaluative measures in this fashion (Bauer and Rhoades 1996; Lewis 1999).

I lectured more frequently as the forms "reinforce[d] the long-held notion that an 'authoritative commanding . . . model' of teaching . . . is the most effective and hence, the most valuable" (Bauer and Rhoades 1996, 96). I increasingly focused on product as opposed to process, and spoon-fed them information they were expected to learn.

Some students of color and Black faculty/staff have also misunderstood my views and politics, but it is important to add that I have received overwhelmingly positive responses from the majority of students of color whom I have taught. Although few in number, they have regularly expressed pleasure about my presence, the issues I raise, and my lack of trepidation in the confrontation of racism.

Yet, these few bright moments dim in the larger picture. While my purpose in the Bronx had been clear, I was much less clear about my mission in this new setting. I knew that most of the teachers entering urban centers were inexperienced, White, female, and culturally out of sync with their students (Gay 1993; Darling-Hammond with Green 1994). I knew that the perpetuation of this dilemma would result in further "dis-education" ("the experience [of] pervasive, persistent and disproportionate underachievement in comparison to their White counterparts") of the Black and Latino masses. I desired to play some role in the transformation of urban education so that it would more directly serve students, their families and communities (Carruthers 1994, 45). Yet, mounting difficulties led me to question my reasons for remaining on this particular campus. I was forced to examine my perspectives as both person and pedagogue. Ellsworth (as quoted in Jipson 1995, 189) suggests that "the relation between teachers/students becomes voyeuristic when the voice of the pedagogue . . . goes unexamined." I am positive that I would not have remained if I had not made significant self-discoveries in the process of thinking about leaving.

I realized that while I understood the relevance of a liberatory peda-gogy for me and the cultures to which I belonged or felt an affinity, I had not yet fully comprehended its significance or relevance for Whites. Dur-ing my early experiences with White students and faculty at the university level, I viewed both bodies monolithically. This view was established as a result of my perceptions of their lack of respect and empathy for me, as well as the antagonism those perceptions generated.

In the long run, students, a few colleagues, and my experiences have helped me to confront assumptions of homogeneity and my tendency to overgeneralize. While I continue to believe the validity of my original claims concerning White students and colleagues' intolerance, I also accept re-sponsibility for committing the same crime (to a certain extent). Pres-ently, I more fully appreciate the issue of diversity, especially as I become more involved in my students' stories.

Once I began to *truly* listen to my students, I heard the stories of marginalization that they shared. This "homogeneous" group became diversified as they spoke of oppression resulting from socioeconomic dif-ference, linguistic barriers, immigrant status, sexual orientation, interra-cial relationships, being parents of biracial children, and transracial adop-tion. Some also talked about the distinct marginality associated with being female.

During my first couple of years at the university, I failed to acknowl-edge that, despite my self-description as a radical teacher, some of the methods I used silenced my students. Although well intentioned, I tended to talk *at* students. For example, I grew tired of my students' racist as-sumptions about their future students, so I spent some time discussing the implications of such assumptions. Yet, why weren't they getting the message? I currently believe that identifying such discrepancies in a di-dactic fashion had proven inefficacious. Such pedantic exercises made students feel guilty and cast me in the role of the multicultural police. While my students are partially responsible for the learning environment created, I am also responsible for creating an atmosphere that was less than conducive for the processes of teaching and learning.

As time has progressed, I have become more confident of my identi-ties as pedagogue and person. Consequently, I have been better able to assist students, by encouraging dialogue and presenting diverse perspec-tives. I now realize that by encouraging the development of student voice and sharing my perspective in a less threatening manner, students are prompted to share in a similar fashion that will, ultimately, benefit their teaching. Additionally, they are encouraged to reexamine their thinking and roles as citizens in an emerging democracy and as teachers, as I am continually in the process of reexamining my own.

While I am no longer presumptuous enough to think that I will change student attitudes that have formed over a lifetime, I do think that I am capable of inspiring students to question their assumptions. I am also teaching them the art of "dissensus," "agreeing to disagree" (Trimbur 1989). Academe should serve as an environment in which intellectual challenge and debate are fostered; a place in which nonconformity and the idiosyncrasy of thought is valued. The role of an intellectual is to encourage the growth of such an environment.

Further, I have realized that, in the past, I have fought academia's racism in a resistant fashion rather than a counter-hegemonic one. Kathleen Weiler, in *Women Teaching for Change: Gender, Class and Power* (1988), distinguishes by stating that "resistance 'is usually informal [and] disorganized' but counter-hegemony implies a more critical theoretical understanding and is expressed in organized and active political opposition" (55).

I would currently characterize my approach to the racism I have described in this essay as counter-hegemonic. It is further described as a "fight back" approach by Reyes and Halcon (1996). They suggest that fighting back may be done in either of two ways. The way that I have selected has been:

> to learn to play the game, without compromising either . . . integrity or ethnicity . . . to comply with the rules only insofar as issues related to scholarship will earn . . . tenure . . . [and focus] attention to minority concerns and minority-related research that will help improve the condition of [the] community (101).

I have learned a lesson that many scholars of color who have gone before me have learned as well, that "survival is not an academic skill" (Lorde 1984, 112). Instead, Lorde characterizes it as:

> learning how to stand alone, unpopular and sometimes reviled, and how to make common cause with those others identified as outside the structures in order to define and seek a world in which we can all flourish (112).

While my discoveries have empowered me and enabled me to survive academia, to some degree, there have been consequential psychic costs. Two weeks after the birth of my daughter, I found myself (in front of the toilet) until dawn. That night, I believed that I would leave my newborn daughter without a mother. By the next night, I had been rushed into surgery with a life-threatening intestinal blockage. It would not be fair to state that my job solely helped me to reach that point. After all, my marriage assisted.

I still trust few and befriend even fewer. I continue to accept limited opportunities to collaborate professionally, preferring to work independently. In essence, I am still a woman without a country on my campus. Yet, to use a description of British Olympian Linford Christie, who refused to leave the track after being disqualified, I consider myself "perfectly balanced . . . [I] have a chip on both shoulders."

Note: Throughout this piece, I use the descriptors "Black," "Latina/o" and "White" consciously and purposefully. The term "Black" was selected as opposed to African American in an attempt to express the deep connection among all of the African Diaspora. The term "Latina/o" is descriptively used to reflect the deep connection among all . . . in the Americas who are descendants of native inhabitants, Spanish, and other European colonizers, and enslaved Africans or any combination of these groups" (Nieto 1992, 177). "White" is used to identify those who have historically benefited from societally privileged "White" skin, both in acknowledged and unacknowledged fashion.

Chapter 3

Voice . . . Muted and Regained

More than four years have elapsed since I started to compose the preceding essay. Since that time, I have become tenured and promoted to the rank of associate professor (two separate processes) at the institution about which I wrote. I have had another baby, divorced, and become a single parent of two children.

In the process of writing this book, I felt the second essay would serve as an appropriate point of departure to a discussion on academia. I believed it would prove beneficial to both me and the potential reader to revisit the issues discussed and reflect upon that particular time in my life.

In rereading and revising the essay, I faced a number of questions. For example, what life experiences have enabled me to survive academia to this point? What strategies have I employed that assist me in coping? What prior life experiences have shaped me as a pedagogue, an emerging intellectual, and a person? What influences have shaped my love of scholarship, intellect, and political activism? Why is my life's work so intimately connected to issues of culture and community? Why do I remain committed to liberatory practice? How have I developed as a literate being?

Dilemmas

Without a doubt, I have been the most conflicted about the writing of this particular essay. It leaves the core of my identity exposed. It makes the details of my life quite public. As I wrote, I continually asked myself if I should reveal so much. In many respects, "writing for me is an act of sacrifice . . . I deliberately sacrifice myself in writing. I leave no part of myself out, for that is how much I want readers to connect with me" (Williams, 1991, 92).

As scholars (a role that encompasses both those of teacher and researcher), we routinely ask people to disclose information about themselves and their identities so that we might more fully understand the world in which we live.

Historically, we have not reciprocated. Thus, the power differential between researcher and "the researched" is maintained and reinforced. In order for researchers to approach research participants in a more empathic and culturally sensitive fashion, we must explore our own lives and unveil our humanity, especially if we expect that courtesy from those we study (Middleton 1993). We must serve as models of reflexivity and critical inquiry.

Further, as a Black researcher, I must take into consideration the ethical dimensions of chronicling the lives of other Blacks, theory-building on Black female epistemology, and speaking about the effects of racism and oppression within and on the Black community without appropriately revealing the ways in which those demons affect me (as a member of the group), as well. bell hooks (1992) persuasively states:

> When contemporary black intellectuals speak about the plight of African Americans, the mounting despair and nihilism, they usually invoke images of a dehumanized underclass ravaged by external and internal genocidal forces. Rarely do any of us, frankly and without shame, dare to name our own struggle to ward off depression, despair, suicidal impulses, and addictions, exposing the reality of our lives . . . We too are in crisis (48).

Through the vehicle of this essay, I have attempted to deviate from this pattern. I have attempted to acknowledge my paradoxical identity as an intellectual, as an "outsider-within" (Collins 1990). The outsider-within perspective is uniquely ascribed to Black Womanist scholars. The position affords us the ability to understand the ramifications of our research and theories for the mainstream. Yet, concomitantly, such status brings understanding regarding the marginality and oppression experienced and related by other Black women, who are also our research participants. Outsider-within status focuses on a "grounding in traditional African American culture [that] provide[s] the material backdrop for a unique Black women's standpoint on self and society. As outsiders-within, Black women have a distinct view of the contradictions between the dominant group's actions and ideologies" (Collins 1990, 11).

I also concluded that I have a responsibility to speak for myself, define my own reality, and present that example to others. Yes, don't get it twisted, the fact that I have lived "this," that each day presents a situation in which I will be denied access in some form or made to feel that I must prove myself, affords me the right to speak for myself. The fact that, previously, Whites have confused the message and subjugated my words provides me with the obligation to tell my own story, in detail. "For Black women, as well as Black men, it is axiomatic that if we do not define ourselves, we will be defined by others - for their use and to our detriment" (Lorde 1984, 45).

In relating my story, I am quite cautious in distinguishing that I do not represent all Black women, though a number of us might share similar issues. Instead, I attempt to delineate the fullness and complexity of my own humanity. This approach is noteworthy because it adds to an existing body of research that documents the plurality and multiple perspectives of Black women. It dispels the myth that there is a singular and unidimensional voice (Marshall 1994; Higginbotham 1982).

In reflecting upon the issue of disclosure, I have also been concerned because the intensely personal nature of this essay involves the sharing of others' lives (those who are closest to me), in addition to my own. Those others have not necessarily agreed to make their lives public, nor might they share the same memories that I do. Some of the memories shared evoke a great deal of pain for me. I anticipate that they will be equally painful for my family to read and remember. As I sit here, I envision that upon reading this essay, my mother will glare at me and say, in her half-joking manner, "Why are you always drudging up this old stuff? I'm goin' to pray for you 'cause you need to give your life to the Lord." My sister will probably say, in her way, "whatever." Yet, I'm confident that we will get past this obstacle, as we have all others, because they are "my peoples" and we understand each other.

I have also thought about the ways in which colleagues and students will respond to me after reading this essay, specifically. I ponder the meaning they will attach to it and the feelings it will evoke. While I am aware that they might feel even more discomfort in their interactions with me as a result of this essay, I also believe that they will be forced to reexamine the ways in which they view the world, in contrast to the ways in which others view it, and contemplate the lenses through which they see people.

Finally, the writing of this essay has been difficult because I am positive that some critic will, in a far too simplistic analysis, characterize the essay as "Black male-bashing." There might be Black male writers who use my words to construct an argument, in an unfortunate choice of words, that I am yet another "barking dog." These words have been used to describe other Womanist writers. There will be others who contend that I have appeased White audiences by "putting Black men down."

As the mother of a son who I desire will grow with a healthy self-concept and a daughter who I hope will see men as her equals, no better or no worse, I would not consciously seek to "bash" those to whom I feel a very deep and special connection. In my estimation, this essay charts a journey of which Black men have played notable roles. It describes a particular set of experiences. I have attempted to speak the truth as I have lived it. While I do not view Black men as a monolith and I recognize individuality, I document *my* interpretations and perceptions. This story is not one of victimization. It is one of triumph. To use my aunt's words, I define triumph as "I am still standing and relatively sane." I will not let anticipated criticisms paralyze me. Too many Black women's narratives have been lost this way. Too many Black women's voices have been muted.

Beginnings

During the year of my birth, 1964, Martin Luther King, Jr. received the Nobel Peace Prize, and the bodies of Chaney, Schwerner, and Goodman, three civil rights workers, were found in Mississippi. It seemed as though the world were in the process of upheaval. People of color, as well as Whites committed to racial justice and social change, had found their collective voice once again. Change was demanded rather than requested.

I was born in a Bronx-based hospital to a "Southern girl," to use the words of Erykah Badu. Though she arrived in New York at 19 and has remained in the tri-state area (New York, New Jersey, and Connecticut) ever since, my mother is a native of Birmingham, Alabama. Her memories of Birmingham include strong familial and community ties; not knowing that her family was poor because they gave to the needy, "only to discover that we were the needy," and being the first family on the block with a television, so her friends came to my grandparents' home and pretended they were at the movies.

There are also memories of times during which the "earth shook." Later, she would discover that the church standing opposite her house had been bombed. Other recollections include the day in which my mother and other neighborhood children looked on as a band of White police officers shot their neighbor dead after he beat his wife for the last time. He stood, drunk and staggering, in his underwear with a butcher knife raised over his head. Minutes later, he fell from the numerous shots targeted at him.

My earliest recollections of my mother focus on her example as "a doer," as was her mother before her. A "doer" is someone who is committed to the enhancement of community, in addition to self-actualization (Etter-Lewis 1993). I remember my mother going to work. I vividly recall my mother working after school with children who needed extra help, attending graduate school to obtain her master's in the evenings and some Saturdays, going to the library, and holding study sessions in our home. From early in life, I had a very clear understanding concerning the magnitude of education and service.

My mother was my champion. She was my protector, the one who believed in me and fought for me. Many people talk about my mother's quiet, soft-spoken, and traditionally Southern demeanor. I do not know her as such. If anyone treated my sister or me unfairly, my mother was "in their face," "getting them told," confronting and questioning in a quiet, but forceful manner. Though she maintained decorum in school and with my teachers, my mother was not afraid to curse people out. She refused to be dismissed or ignored. I was always exceedingly proud of my mother's competence and confidence. She seemed fearless, and I loved when she stood up for me.

Education as a Value

My mother emphasized the best possible education for both my sister and me, as she did the love of family. An example of my mother's level of commitment toward this end was her sole responsibility in transitioning me, with very little money, from the public schools of New York City to an exclusive boarding school in Massachusetts through the *A Better Chance* program. The *ABC* program (as it is called) places exemplary students from traditionally marginalized cultures in school settings to which they might not otherwise be exposed. My mother knew about the program as a result of her role within the New York City public school system. My school's guidance counselor had not mentioned nor distributed applications for the program. When I asked the first time, he told me that he had misplaced them and had no idea where they could be found. My mother sent notes requesting the application. He put me off several times more before I returned to his office, in tears. I was less fearful of being a pest than I was of returning home that day without the application. Through her persistence, my mother was responsible for assisting me and two of my classmates to gain program acceptance.

My maternal grandmother routinely spoke with me about the power of education and the importance of college, as well. College was never a second thought in my family; I would graduate as had my mother, uncle, and aunt. I would acquire a master's degree as they all had, as well. I believe that higher education was so important to my grandmother because she never received the opportunity to finish. Her duties as wife and mother precluded it. That experience led to the stern warning: "If you have your education, when these men start to act up, you can leave and still take care of yourself." This warning has turned into a self-fulfilling prophecy. I believe that my grandmother also felt the message was warranted because I was perpetually "fast." From very early in life, I loved boys and I was good at attracting the "wrong types."

Nana's commitment to my education also translated into action. When I went to college, my mother, my sister, my grandparents, and I traveled from Birmingham to the University of Alabama in Tuscaloosa. It soon became evident that my mother, who was divorced and struggling for the second time, did not have all of my tuition, especially as they added various "fees" of which she was unaware. When we went back to Birmingham, Nana got up early the next morning and disappeared until noon. She arrived home with all of the needed tuition money.

The Personal Power of Literacy

As a little girl, I spoke up. I was always talking and I talked more than I should. I also wanted to know more than was considered good for me. Thus, I probably had the makings of a Womanist early in life. I knew no boundaries in terms of those things that should remain private and those that were fit for public consumption. I questioned, challenged, and failed to comprehend secrecy. A constant admonition from my mother was, "What happens in this house stays in this house. Do you understand?" For the most part, I did not and I still don't. Further, in my home, truth was important. You would get a whipping for lying quicker than for any other offense. Thus, I valued truth. I believe that my facility with spoken language led to subsequent facility with that which is written.

I always recall having books in my life and loving stories. Some of my earliest and fondest memories include my grandparents reading picture storybooks to me that my mother had sent. Then, the books served as the lifeline between my mother and me as we were temporarily separated and I lived with my grandparents. I remember sitting on my grandmother's lap (or my mother's when she visited). I can still feel my mother's and grandmother's skin against my own and the smell of their perfume and warm breath. Thus, for me, the affective qualities of those readings were as consequential as the content.

Upon returning home to live with my mom, I was also introduced to story (in another form) by my godmother. She cared for me as my mother worked. I was homeschooled during pre-K and kindergarten, for the most part. In the morning, my godmother taught me the alphabet, numbers, colors, and other concepts. Yet, we spent many weekday afternoons crocheting and looking at her "stories" or soap operas. We looked at *The Guiding Light, As the World Turns,* and others. If she left temporarily to prepare lunch or start dinner, it was my job to recount the tales.

My godmother also loved movie musicals. Thus, we passed a number of evenings watching and discussing the beauty of *The King and I, The Flower Drum Song* or *Carousel,* with her providing greater ambiance as she described the experience of viewing a number of the shows live on Broadway. When I was fortunate enough to spend New Year's Eve with her, we would watch the late movie, she would drink champagne, and I would drink a concoction she had manufactured that consisted of grape juice and ginger ale.

I still spent summers in Birmingham where I loved the fresh air, sunshine, and freedom. I also loved the time that I spent reading and watching old movies.

Throughout my childhood, reading proved a site of tremendous competence for me. My mother and grandmother were continually surprised by the number of books that I was able to complete and discuss within a relatively brief period of time. I loved the language of books, as well as the use and beauty of big words. I received great pleasure from having an extensive collection of words at my command. Yet, this command of language also distanced me from others, both in school and outside of it. I distinctly remember instances of throwing "big" words around as I ate with my babysitter and her two daughters, or correcting Miss Gladys's mispronunciations. I usually went on, at a great rate, until finally "Miss Gladys" looked at me and said, in an apropos fashion, " Shut up, Dedrin. It's not nice to use words that other people don't understand just for the sake of usin' them."

Literacy, books, and popular culture remained steadfast friends, though my life took a vastly different turn.

A Voice Muted

Though my mother was confident and competent when it came to protecting my sister and I from "the world," those qualities did not translate in her relationships with men. The relationships I remember best were those she had with my father and my stepfather. Both relationships ended in divorce. I viewed both men as wild, intelligent, flashy, controlling, and attractive. A lamentable outcome of my mother's relationships has been that, with few exceptions, I have been passionately drawn to the same type.

Exempting my grandfather, these are the type of men I know best. I attract and am attracted to the familiar. With these men, a strange dance between pleasure and danger takes place to which I have been addicted; though I actively struggle toward health, more so for my children than for myself. Though I have been attracted to and dated a few White men, I have had a lifetime of love-hate relationships with Black men. The importance of this point lies in the fact that I do not address any inherent flaws in Black men. Instead, I point to the fact that I have been attracted to a certain kind of Black man and that attraction has frequently led to my subsequent victimization.

While my stepfather exacted his wrath primarily on my mother, my father was abusive to everyone in the house. Abusive episodes were usually the result of my mother "talking back," questioning a decision made, or failing to give detailed accounts of her whereabouts.

My father was intensely controlling. He was verbally abusive to my sister. I will not go into his abuse of me, except to say that his weapons of choice were powerful verbal assaults (like "I can't understand why you are so fucking stupid. I know you didn't get that from me" or "My belief is you're gonna grow up and be a lesbian"), and sexual threats. The scars left have not been physical. They have been deep and psychological. In many respects, they remain with me to this day.

With both of my mother's long-term relationships, life was chaotic. There were usually frightening eruptions and then calm. Thus, I grew up valuing peace and expecting disequilibrium and violence. For this reason, I find arguments about the effects of media violence on children alarming and extremist. While I find some validity in claims that children become desensitized to violence with heightened exposure via television, movies, radio, and video games, I am much more concerned about the violence that children actually experience directly in their homes.

It is also for this reason that I have difficulty with a contention made by some dysfunctional couples. According to them, they remain together for the sake of the children. What lessons do children truly learn about love, marriage, and family from parents who don't even like each other? What do they learn about truth and personal fulfillment? There are other lessons that I believe they do, in fact, learn. They learn a great deal about deceit, disrespect, and rage.

Once the abuse commenced, I learned to use words in a manner that I had not previously employed, for the purpose of obfuscating the truth. I lied in an effort to conceal. My mother did not. After an incident in which my stepfather had punched her in the eye with a force that chipped her eye socket, my mother's eye was so swollen and purple that people who came to our home would ask, "What happened to you?" My mother proclaimed, without flinching or looking embarrassed, "I didn't duck soon enough" as my stepfather averted our visitors' gaze. When physicians asked, "How did this happen?" My mother smiled and said "a fist" as my stepfather looked on. Yet, I lied.

If I missed school after a bout, I told my teachers, who didn't necessarily ask about the absence, that I had to remain home because my mother fell on my skates. I don't think any of them cared enough to believe that there might be more to such a story. After all, I was one of the quiet ones. I didn't make trouble and, within the New York City public school system, that quality restated led to neglect.

During this period, I stopped speaking up, as well. Instead, I read and enjoyed popular culture (movies, television, and the radio) even more. I read primarily to escape pain. Through books, voice was given to my thoughts. They were companions that eased loneliness and were used to insulate me. They helped to stabilize my world.

In school, I was different from other girls. I was always asked to read aloud and my writing was prized. I was also painfully shy and aloof. In many respects, I remain this way today. I have become intimately familiar with the truth Lorraine Hansberry spoke as she wrote, "Eventually it comes to you, the thing that makes you exceptional, if you are at all, is inevitably that which must also make you lonely" (1969, 148).

The distinctions I've mentioned, along with socioeconomic status issues, served to estrange me from others. Specifically, my family was middle-class and my classmates were poor and working-class. While my mother privileged education and family, she was not necessarily concerned that I wear "the latest style" or have the freedom "to hang out" with friends. Thus, in many respects, I was socially distanced from my peers. I believe that my classmates viewed me (as an extension of my family) as stuck-up and elitist, in spite of the fact that I admired and wished to emulate them.

Outside of school, I had similar issues. I often preferred books to people. Reading transported me when there were social gatherings at which I felt inept and out of place.

Additionally, books provided me with answers that adults weren't able to give. In fact, I found out about menstruation from a book that my mother handed me, saying, "if you have any questions, ask me." At other junctures, my mother and her aunt spoke late into the night during our weekend sojourns to Yonkers, while I spent hours (unbeknownst to them) pouring over *Everything you always wanted to know about sex, but were afraid to ask* and *The Hite Report.* They were the most fascinating reads ever for an eleven year old. Even back then, I loved using literacy for my own purposes and I hated the way it was approached in school.

Beauty As a Commodity

Literacy also helped me to escape feelings of inadequacy. I grew up in a household in which beauty was the commodity. While I had loved my mother's intervening for me because I valued her strength, I also loved others' expressions of surprise to discover that I belonged to my mother. After all, she was so "strikingly beautiful." My mother remains tall, stunning, and distinctive. Routinely, people comment on her green eyes, thick hair, and keen features.

My younger sister has been praised all of her life, also, for her light skin and thick, wavy hair. To this day, I joke with her, telling her that I don't like going any place with her. It takes us so long to get where we're going with men chasing after her, yelling "hey, light-skinned." People ask her on a regular basis if she is biracial and/or which of her parents is White.

Conversely, there was me. I was merely "the smart one," as society doesn't seem to value little, skinny, brown-skinned girls with glasses. Yet, adolescence was both kind and cruel to me. I developed early and found that many men were attracted to me. Though I had not yet experienced sex, I often mistook men's sexual pursuit of me for love and erroneously viewed their lust as kindness. It is odd, but I recently discovered that I am still prone to such mistakes.

Soon after, however, I developed a case of chicken pox at thirteen. The effects were devastating, for the routine childhood disease left symmetrical keloids, thick raised scars, on both sides of my face, in addition to my right shoulder. Life is hard enough for adolescent, Black girls; but, this situation merely compounded the problems. I became even more withdrawn because of the scars, thinking that if I didn't draw too much attention to myself by speaking out, people would not notice or ask me about them.

I find it ironic that the keloids serve as a metaphor. I frequently mask emotional scars. Yet, I am clearly unable to hide those that are physical. They serve as a road map of my life in some ways. They have greatly affected daily living. From that time to this, I have lived with a condition that I consider debilitating, to a certain extent. I rarely volunteer information about the keloids or divulge my feelings about them, unless I am asked directly or I am in the company of family or close friends.

They cause me to disconnect myself from others. For instance, I will flinch if someone relatively unfamiliar rests a hand on my shoulder. While I believe that this reaction adds to the view that I am standoffish, aloof, and detached, it is my manner of protecting myself.

Though they have been removed, they have returned, enlarged (with two pregnancies), and others have formed, I have been, grudgingly, forced to learn to accept this aspect of myself, as well as the fact that my body rebels against itself and heals in this fashion.

Others have asked, as if to appease me, if I realize the power of the gifts that have been bestowed upon me, those of intellect and expression. I frequently smile when I hear this, for women's intellect is not prized in this society. We live in a world that penalizes women for intellect rather than celebrates them. Smart women and artists are, most frequently, said to be crazy.

I reflect upon being much younger and reading Bronte's *Jane Eyre*. I remember how angry I was at Mrs. Rochester. After all, she was a pain in the ass, messing up Jane's life and getting in the way of others' happiness. Only later, did it dawn on me that it was Mrs. Rochester's life that was being fucked up. Her husband locked her in an attic and he was pursuing another woman in her midst.

I also think about my gravitation to the movie *Fatal Attraction* and some of my feminist colleagues' reactions when I name it as a favorite movie. It remains so, for I never view Alex as crazy and out of control, though she may be. I view her as seeing clearly enough to realize that she was being used and attempting to alter the power differential in her favor. "I have grown to womanhood in a world where the saner you are, the madder you are made to appear" (Gwaltney 1980, 7).

I am also led to think of Morrison's *Beloved*, whose protagonist Sethe, is a fictionalized portrait of Margaret Garner, a slave woman who killed her infant daughter and drowned another of her children as she attempted suicide in response to the oppressive and dehumanizing forces of slavery. I have sat through many a session (that leave my ears burning with anger) with Whites claiming to have insight into the Black experience and verbally masturbating with their progressive and liberal thought, asking how one does such a thing. I have no problem envisioning the point at which one sees murder and suicide as viable retorts to oppression. Why? Because I, like my sisters Mrs. Rochester, Alex, Sethe, and Margaret, am crazy.

Writing was another venue of expression during this tumultuous period. The use of paper and pencil was as liberating as reading. It was also during this time, in high school, that I was first published. The first piece that received a great deal of attention from my teachers was about life in prison. My mother was critical of the piece because she was concerned that I was writing about that with which I had no experience. Little did she know that I had experience. I had lived within the prison of domestic violence, the prison of my body, which I felt betrayed the beauty and depth of my soul. I also lived in the prison of a new environment, hundreds of miles away from home . . . a prison in which Whiteness and wealth, neither of which I had, were privileged. Thus, at home, I didn't have the valued capital, beauty, and in this new arena, once again I was missing the capital that would make me a player. Quite clearly, I was imprisoned.

A Voice Recovered

As my "voice" had left with trauma, it was restored in the same fashion. Domestic violence had taught me to lie, appear unobtrusive, keep my thoughts to myself, and remain quiet. Further, my mother's relationship with my stepfather taught me that the use of wit and intellect, "talking back," could prompt a slap. In this fashion, I learned some long-lasting lessons about womanhood. If one followed the rules of true "womanhood," she would be safe and avoid violence.

This false sense of security was shattered during my first few months at college. After being on campus a short while, I was courted by a 6'4" football player whom many women "wanted." Though he pretended that he was only minimally interested in me, he often appeared at events he knew I was attending and would become volatile if I was speaking with a man, any man. I loved him completely and lost my virginity to him at sixteen. I believe that he sensed an incredible vulnerability in me that he found very attractive. If I attempted to leave the relationship, he would pull out his trump card and promise to marry me.

It was also with this man that I experienced the violence and terror of rape, as he and one of his fraternity brothers exposed me to the act early one January morning. The experience was terrifying and I recall feeling both under siege and terribly alone. I remember a rape that was physical and mental as my "fiancé" attempted to convince me that the incident never occurred. Alternately, I had imagined it or I had wanted it.

The details are stark and brutal. Yet, I do not reveal details of the rape because I do not wish to set a voyeuristic trap for readers, leading them to focus on misuses of power that masquerade as raw, carnal, sex acts. I also do not want the reader to associate the details with Black men, giving any credence to claims made by scholars like Susan Brownmiller (1975) and Jean MacKellar (1975) that men of color are prone to sexual violence.

The importance of relating the rape lies in the fact that the experience dispelled a myth. I had followed all the rules of "womanhood," I had kept my mouth shut, suppressed my intellect, and I had still been victimized. While I had not caused my rape, my passivity and fear had made me a willing participant in my own abuse.

I was forced to reevaluate my self-imposed silence. Further, I was forced to speak up, return to truth, and reclaim my voice. I also found it interesting that I had to now assume the torch that my mother had carried for me. I now had to speak for myself. This point was most evident as my mother stayed with me for a few days to help me through the crisis. She cautioned that it might be best to let the matter drop, especially as the police stated that my assailant couldn't truly be prosecuted. After all, I was involved in a relationship with him and I voluntarily went to his residence. To me, this explanation sounded very much like "you got what you deserved." Additionally, I made the mental leap that it might have been acceptable, in the eyes of these men, for him to kill me. Their looks also revealed quite directly that "I was just another Black whore." I distinguish my use of the term "Black whore" in the following fashion. Through the lens of the mainstream, many Black women "whore as a way of being, as an innateness of sootiness and contamination, as a sticky-sweet inherency of black womanhood" (Williams 1991, 175).

Yet, I decided to pursue it as a university disciplinary infraction. I testified alone, I faced my "fiancé" and confronted him with the truth. Ultimately, I was responsible for his expulsion from that university. Afterward, I made the decision to remain on campus and graduate, in spite of the fact that most students knew what had occurred, and various versions of the story circulated.

I almost flunked out of school. My approach was to attend only those classes I found interesting on a regular basis. All others, I attended just frequently enough to pass. While I failed to attend those classes that were "boring" to me until my grade had reached the critical point, I consistently attended those which privileged literature, writing, Black subject matter, and feminism. I loved viewing the world through the multiple and contradictory lenses presented in many of these courses. For me, they were freeing and emancipatory.

There was no one truly to talk with, even though I eventually made two close friends with whom I have remained in contact. My mother's look when I raised the subject of my rape told me that it was never to be discussed again. I was harassed by my assailant's frat brothers. Their favorite names for me were derivations of "bitch." Well-intentioned men and women took it upon themselves to tell subsequent men I dated that I had "fucked this guy and his friend" and with incredulity, they added, "and Nigger got expelled because of it." I was the persecutor. Frequently, I was forced to make the disclosure before others did.

Once again, paper and pencil, books, and popular culture media rescued me. I wrote about my experiences in my varied journals. For me, the initial process of writing was cathartic. I worked things out and made sense of what had occurred on paper. I also commenced writing for the campus newspaper and was published routinely. Eventually, I was even offered my own column. It was on this terrain that I first commenced to use my writing to make change. The most influential change resulted from my exposure of an incident during which a young, Black, female acquaintance (a new admit to the university) was asked to leave a White frat party. Though we had informed her, on numerous occasions, that fraternities and sororities were divided across lines of race, she still decided to go because a group of White female friends had asked her.

To my surprise, the Black community rallied behind me and I became a celebrity because of my courage this time. Yet, the Whites on campus were clearly upset by the allegation of racism, as well as my public "outing" of the fraternity. At one point, their faculty advisor called me into his office and closed the door. He warned me that I was "asking for trouble by slandering these boys." My response was "bring it then," as a I gathered my belongings and left.

I was amazed that others could be so moved to action by my words; words that I had selected and positioned. At this point in time, it is clear that the rebellious spirit that I possessed early in life had returned.

The Present

Many of the life lessons learned during college have remained with me, in addition to those, taught by my mother, grandmother, and godmother. Today, I would characterize myself as still quiet and distant, but I also have a rebellious and wild spirit. I don't like restrictions nor attempts to control me. I do "my own thing."

In sharing this chapter with several colleagues and friends, the descriptor "painful" keeps coming to the surface. I have been told a number of times that it presents a "painful read." Yet, recently a good friend who was critiquing the essay stated, with a thoughtful and nonplused look on her face, "Dierdre, this chapter bothers me. Why might people want to know this about you?"

This question has run through my thoughts at frequent intervals. I have asked myself about the essay's purpose and connection to the other essays. In response, I present this essay, with the others, as a model of constructivism and praxis. "It is a reflection on action, informed by active struggle and in turn informing that struggle . . . it is double-voiced, expressing the ambiguity of those who know the experience of belonging and not belonging" (Lawrence 1995, 337).

Through a genre which some have described as closely resembling memoir, I have attempted to discuss the way in which past experiences shape present reality. I desire to outline the way in which we all construct our own realities and the means by which key life events affect the development of identity. In a related manner, I have wished to provide examples which illustrate the paradoxical struggle among the positionalities of race, gender, and class that many Black women experience. Very early in life, I was forced into the process of making sense of the concentric spheres of race, class, and gender and learning to cope with them relationally.

In my estimation, the story that I have related on these pages is nothing extraordinary. Unfortunately, many Black girls grow up with parallel realities. Current statistics suggest that most Black children grow up in homes in which a father is not present. As a result, many of those children (although not all) grow up without knowing positive Black male role models. Making the case specific to Black girls, if a young girl grows up without such models, she might have a difficult time identifying positive traits in a potential partner. The process becomes an exercise in trial and error that can, sometimes, prove detrimental.

As a defense mechanism, we are socialized to be self-reliant and independent because we receive the message, in word, image, and deed, that we cannot depend upon Black men (Chapman 1995; Joseph 1991). We are frequently taught to fixate on flaws, highlighting their irresponsibility, emotional unavailability, cruelty, and abuse. In a similar fashion, Black men are socialized to view us as the enemy, as conspiring with Whites in their destruction, or at least some Black male authors and social critics, like Ishmael Reed and Tony Brown, have accused us of such deeds. They rely upon images of us as controlling, domineering (Chapman, 1995), devious, and "with mad attitude."

A hapless outcome of our joint dependency on these images is our roles in the reinforcement of our colonization. Possibly, it is easier to blame each other than to work against the effects that slavery's ravages have wreaked on our institutions (e.g., marriage, families, socioeconomic self-sufficiency) (Patterson 1998; Chapman 1995).

I have also used this essay as a vehicle through which to transgress borders. In deciding to reveal my rape, I have had to cope with the realization that this traumatizing act was committed by Black men. I believe that, like many Black women who have experienced such trauma at the hands of Black men, I was obligated to confront my fear that revealing such an experience would embarrass me (because of its sexual nature) and leave me open to the criticism that I was being disloyal to Black men.

An especially ironic twist for a number of Black women who relate incidents focusing on Black men's victimization of us is the condemnation sometimes heaped on us by other Black women (Chapman 1995). At times, our "sisters" attack most vehemently; calling our womanhood, intellect, Blackness, and even dignity into question. According to this group's conceptualization, I guess "real" Black women grit their teeth and bear abuse. I suggest that Black women, collectively, revisit this expectation and our plausible collusion in an oppression that proves deleterious and divisive to us all.

In too many instances, rape survivors are made to feel that we should be ashamed. *We should not.* Those who, of whichever hue, use sex as a weapon of domination and terror should be made to feel shame. It is also important for White women to understand that Black women are left in pain and devastation, too, after rape.

Additionally, as I searched for appropriate Black female mentors as a young Black woman coming into maturity and womanhood, I tended to distance myself from such women, believing that they had never experienced the feelings and unspoken horrors that I had. I use the term *mentor* consciously in this essay and distinguish between role models and mentors. "The word 'mentor' has an intellectual connotation . . . Because mentors provide some intellectual guidance, they must be respected intellectually" (T. L. Banks 1995, 329).

In my readings about them and conversations, I never had a real sense of their lives. At this point, I understand the reasoning behind such lack of disclosure. It is incredibly risky. Primarily, the peril rests upon the tenuous place of Black female intellectuals in this society and the way in which our work is so summarily dismissed. In an effort to dispel fallacious myths about us, many choose against revealing aspects of themselves that might be perceived as damaging credibility or reinforcing the view of Black women as body rather than brain. In my quest to provide young Black women with another potential mentor, I affirm that I am both brain and body. I am affected by the same forces that affect women across lines of race, class, and sexual orientation. Yet, I am also empathic with Black men as we, often, fight together for dignity and equality in a world that seems intent on denying us those rights.

Chapter 4

The Perplexities of Black Scholarship

On Thursday, March 25, 1999, I got dressed, left my children with my sister, and went to jail.

I was arrested at approximately 11:15 A.M. Primarily, I was arrested because I failed to respond to requests that I remove myself from the entrance of One Police Plaza in Manhattan.

That day, I stood with a diverse group in respect to gender, race, ethnicity, socioeconomic status, and sexual orientation. Yet, we remained in solidarity. We were arrested, together, in protest of the Amadou Diallo shooting in the Bronx. Amadou Diallo, an unarmed African immigrant, was murdered by a group of New York Police Department (NYPD) officers, members of the notorious Street Crimes Unit. At the time of this crime, Street Crimes officers were distinguished from other officers as they wore plain clothes (frequently jeans, sweatshirts, and T-shirts). Additionally, they were infamous for the slogan, "we own the night."

On a winter night, four officers fired a barrage of forty-one bullets at a terrified, 5'3" young, Black man for whom English was a second language. The significance of this notable detail regarding potential language barriers lies in the officers' contention that Diallo failed to respond to commands they allegedly directed toward him.

Since the initial writing of this chapter, the venue for the trial of the four officers was changed from the Bronx to Albany and they were acquitted of all charges. Also, the Bronx District Attorney Robert Johnson, a Black man, is under fire for his perceived mismanagement of the Diallo case.

Though Diallo's murder was the primary motivation for the demonstration, I (like others) thought of the incident as one in a long list of injustices involving the criminal justice system and committed against people of color. I thought of countless others, among them Eleanor Bumpurs (a grandmother whose apartment was stormed by seven NYPD officers during an attempt to illegally evict her, she was shot and killed over $96.85 in back rent), Anthony Baez (a young Latino who was killed as he was placed in a choke hold by an NYPD officer for failing to move a street football game in a timely fashion), Assata Shakur (Joanne Chesimard), Angela Davis, Geronimo Pratt, Leonard Peltier, Mumia Abu-Jamal, and Abner Louima (a Haitian immigrant, who was badly beaten and had a stick shoved into his rectum in a police precinct bathroom by a NYPD officer).

I have also thought, frequently, about my son (a toddler) and wondered if DWB (Driving While Black) might still be an offense punishable by death when he grows up.

By all accounts, we were treated courteously by the NYPD. After all, they could not afford yet another incident, especially with a group of peaceful demonstrators. Also, a number of high-profile figures like Jesse Jackson, Kwiesi Mfume, Ossie Davis, Ruby Dee, and Susan Sarandon had been arrested as well; thus, media attention was focused on the daily protests.

During processing, I was politely informed that my belongings would remain with me as a courtesy that wasn't ordinarily extended. I was also asked if my handcuffs were too tight. Though I indicated that they were not, our arresting officer explained that he'd attempt to make them as loose as possible, but they had to be tight enough for restriction of movement.

Later that afternoon, I was placed with a group of women (among them, a number of Episcopalian priests and seminary students). We were loaded into a paddy wagon and taken to a holding facility. After a short and quite bumpy ride, we were placed in a cell.

For more than an hour, we passed candy, talked, prayed, and sang. During processing, officers called us by our first names and loudly announced our ages most specifically, as well as other bits of personal information. One officer gruffly snickered as another (sitting next to him) read the "Dr." in front of my name. The other women and me shared additional information about our ages, stations in life, and what had brought us to jail that day.

There were two women among us, however, whose quiet presence and dignity remain transfixed in my mind. One was a woman obviously suffering from the ravages of cancer. She was nearly bald and those with whom she came were careful to let officers know that she was experiencing the effects of chemotherapy, so she should be allowed to eat the snacks she brought with her and use the bathroom as needed. In spite of her own circumstances, she was able to see beyond herself and *act* on behalf of another.

Then, there was a priest named Angela. A mass of dreadlocks framed her thin and angular face. After a while, it became evident that she was being treated differently from the rest of us. The treatment was not harsh, it simply signified that she was in more "trouble" than we were. She soon told us that this arrest was her second for the same cause; thus, the officers had informed her that she would spend the night in the "Tombs" where they could not guarantee her safety. I still hear the melodious and lilting quality of her voice and see the fall of her dreadlocks as she said, "It's a minor sacrifice. Others have endured worse for me."

For much of the afternoon, I remained quiet. I spoke only when spoken to, though I smiled frequently and affirmed that which others shared. I have become accustomed to the fact that such is my way. Much of my time was spent deep in thought.

I reflected upon my status, statistically. I met the profile of a female prisoner. Forty-six percent of all women in state prisons are Black and fifty percent are between the ages of 25 and 34. Seventy-eight percent of all women in prison are mothers (Siegal 1998). The realization that "there, but for the grace of God, go I" was jarring and disconcerting.

Further, I contrasted the treatment received by myself and the other "ladies" (as the officers referred to us) with that endured by other Black and brown people who are on "lock down" nationally. For this group, there, traditionally, has been very little courtesy extended and even less regard for comfort. There is not the benefit of counsel, like that afforded me by a colleague from the campus Legal Studies department, who will walk one through the procedure and provide the names of several contacts in the event that a problem ensues.

Most prominently, I thought of my children, who I left with my sister voluntarily that morning to follow my own convictions. As I sat in jail, assured that I would be released in time for dinner, my mind was at ease. I knew, unequivocally, that I would be reunited with my children *that* day. I also knew that they were in strong and capable hands. I was not compelled to accept an ugly reality often faced by women processed through the penal system . . . that social services would "intervene" and "take" my children. If I wanted my children returned after jail time, I would probably be forced to "prove myself," or I would be obligated to think fast of some relative who *might* take my children in.

Though I consider myself as always empathic in respect to the oppressed and our plight, this experience heightened my sensitivity to the point that I was driven to act further. I was also inspired by Angela Davis's Prison Abolition Movement.

Specifically, Davis states that there are those people in society who are violent and should not reside with the rest of us. Yet, the majority of those in jail are there for nonviolent offenses. In fact, ninety-two percent of women prisoners are imprisoned for nonviolent transgressions (Siegal 1998). According to Davis, "Drug offenses and other nonviolent crimes that women commit are often linked to persistent poverty and biased law enforcement practices in low income communities of color" (Siegal 1998, 68).

Many attribute this upsurge in the number of women arrested, convicted, and imprisoned to the Rockefeller mandatory drug sentencing laws. In 1986, Congress passed a new set of minimum penalties for commerce in illegal drugs. While the new laws were supposedly enacted to crackdown on "kingpins," they have been most successful in prosecuting low-level drug offenders, particularly women. Frequently, arrests are intricately linked to issues of substance abuse and/or dysfunctional relationships with men who are trafficking in drugs. Thus, in many respects, the women are being penalized for their own marginality, as related to issues of gender, race, and class. The U.S. war on drugs and mandatory minimum sentencing statutes are partially responsible for the sixfold growth in the number of women housed in prisons, according to a news article in *The New York Times*, 18 August 1997.

One outcome of my own disquietude about my brief jail stay was an initiation of work with women inmates at the Bergen County Jail in Hackensack, New Jersey.

A View Through a Different Prism

The work began with a presentation for the women on literacy development strategies and parenting skills they could plausibly implement with their children. Prior to the visit, I had accepted the jail's terms that I would serve in the capacity of a volunteer and I would not be paid for my services. I prepared an appropriate "talk," keeping in mind that the women were temporarily separated from their children. The morning of the presentation, I loaded up with my usual set of picture books and handouts on brightly colored paper.

I worked from the premise that the workshop participants would be reunited with their children or they would have others, at some point in the future. I had anticipated that I would start sessions as I usually did.

Participants would shape the workshop by voicing their concerns and expressing their needs.

I arrived at the jail at 12:45 P.M., as I was to meet the facilitator of the parenting group at one. I, along with other visitors, was not actually admitted until 1:15. I guess this delayed entry keeps one mindful of the sign prominently displayed that "visiting is a privilege." I mentioned the wait to Gina, the facilitator. She said it was commonplace for visitors to be admitted late. We both chuckled as I, sarcastically, asked if there was such a delay at the conclusion of visiting hours.

I had envisioned that the women would be waiting, for some reason. Yet, at 1:30, they had not arrived and I was steadily becoming more anxious. What if they didn't wish to come? What if they were hostile to the information I presented? I asked Gina if we should reschedule. She calmly responded that we should wait a little longer to see how many actually came. In an effort to avoid confusion, it is noteworthy to mention that I am perpetually nervous about presentations, no matter how many I do. Some of the most tense and hostile have been conducted with White teachers. I would choose to postpone all of them, if I could. Thus, my request was not based on the composition of this particular group.

Soon after, a group of ten or eleven entered the classroom in which Gina and I sat. I was instantly relieved. I smiled as they entered. Many of the women appeared reserved. They seemed uncertain as to my identity or the way in which they should respond to my presence. I had a visceral reaction as I looked at the deep green jumpsuits that they wore and observed that the majority of the women were Black.

A great deal of national attention has been focused on the astronomical rise in the number of Black men currently involved in the criminal justice system and factors that have fostered the increase. The vision before my eyes that day attested to the fact that women generally, and Black women specifically, have a problem of equivalent magnitude.

While I resist the temptation of oversimplifying and claiming that the one hundred twenty-six percent increase in the number of Black women arrested is more significant, I will state that it is commensurably exceptional. In reiteration, statistics suggest that seventy-eight percent of all women in prison are mothers. Since mothers are often described as their children's first teachers, what might these women's children learn from them? Is it possible that, among other lessons, some will learn the same disempowerment and disenfranchisement that led their mothers to prison? Others might learn that survival comes at a tremendously high cost. Exponentially, the dilemma involving imprisoned women is momentous.

Though I quite clearly had an agenda and a plan regarding the talk, I found that the women's concerns surpassed "my neat talk." They were concerned about children who were being held over and classified as possessing "special needs." They desired to devise feasible plans for connecting with children who had been "taken" from them. They wanted to discuss the means through which they might secure contact visits with their children rather than having glass partitions separate them.

This group of women asked questions about understanding bureaucracies and operating strategically in navigating them, from positions of strength. They talked about the use of literacy, via letters, telephone communications and face-to-face discussions, in the procurement of their rights. I sat in awe. I admired their individual, as well as collective, strength and beauty. I appreciated the viable solutions they offered each other and the problem-solving strategies in which they engaged together. I viewed them as "organic intellectuals," a term coined by Antonio Gramsci. Organic intellectuals are defined as those "whose philosophy emerges from an understanding of the common sense world and the historical and economic forces which have shaped it"(Weiler 1988, 15).

Gina and I merely served to fill in blanks. More specifically, I was able to help them, in some instances, to connect their observations with theory and research. For example, we discussed sophisticated concepts (in general terms) like Howard Gardner's Multiple Intelligences Theory, intelligence as fluid rather than static, Ray Rist's study on teacher expectation, and bureaucratic literacy as disempowering.

I found it endearing that the women were concerned about the way that I would view them, the impression they would make. This point was evidenced by their admonitions to each other about cursing and "excusing [their] language." They quickly quelled a disagreement that arose for fear that such opportunities to "talk" would be stripped from them. Yet, I was as concerned as they were, regarding the impression I would make on them. As I left the jail that afternoon, my mind was unsettled. I had so many questions and so many thoughts.

Additionally, I left the jail with a desire to document the women's personal histories, especially those of the Black women housed there. I thought about the teachers with whom I work on a daily basis, in relation to the women involved in the criminal justice system. I thought about the ease with which some of my students write off such women and express their beliefs that the women have very little (of worth) to contribute to the lives of their children. I believe that the ease of judgment is spawned from the students' ability to view these women as a nameless, faceless mass, reminiscent of the worst stereotypes of Black women which come to mind. I pondered the negative implications attached to teaching children whose parents and community one doesn't even respect. Is it possible that a child might benefit from such teaching?

As I continued to reflect on the issue, it seemed as if the documentation of these women's stories and the opportunity for both groups (the teachers and women prisoners) to possibly meet and work together, in some capacity, might lead to a deeper acknowledgment of the women's humanity and a potential understanding (on the part of the women) that one can use systems effectively for the purpose of affecting change. For me, the expressed objectives of both groups are similar. They both profess a commitment to children and an interest in child welfare, an aspect of which is education.

Further, I needed and desired to "hear" more of the women's stories. A few of them came up to me at the workshop's conclusion to offer their thanks and share with me. One woman asked me about the length of my employment at Montclair State. Shortly after, she confided that she was a graduate of the institution, had served in the armed forces, and had advanced technological training. She had been one of the first women to speak during the actual workshop and told many joyful stories that clearly indicated her pride in her preadolescent son.

During the course of our brief chat, she added the caveat, "I've made some bad decisions, some poor choices." I assured her that we all do and that no one had the right to judge. This comment, in addition to my obvious engagement in our discussion, seemed to place her at ease. Other women shared intensely personal information during the workshop, as well.

From the women's narratives, I believed that I'd be able to decipher the ways in which literacy was used in their homes prior to their incarceration, in their schooling and education, in the jail, and with bureaucratic, social service agencies. Brandt (as quoted in Key 1998) refers to literacy "as a metacognitive ability—an increasing awareness of and control over the social means by which people sustain discourse, knowledge and reality" (1). It is my contention that the women housed in the Bergen County Jail, like their sisters in urban centers and impoverished rural areas throughout the United States, have never attained full literacy or the political awareness and control that it can bring; thus, they have been unable to navigate systems and bureaucracies effectively and, in some respects, their disempowerment has led to their incarceration (Collins 1990). "Forbidding Black women to vote, excluding African-Americans and women from public office and withholding equitable treatment in the criminal justice system all substantiate the political subordination of Black women" (Collins 1990, 6).

I also wanted to analyze the ways in which Black women within the penal system construct and use knowledge about womanhood, mothering, and survival. For example, one of the women was concerned because she had recently informed her "man" that she would not return to him, after she left jail. An outcome of her announcement was his threat to take her children. She related his confidence that he would secure custody (based on her incarceration) and asked the group for help. Gina and I immediately thought of the ways in which she could make the court system and social service agencies work for her. Probably, the end result would be her ability to keep her children. One of the other women inmates, however, took a different approach that I found fascinating and equally plausible. She told her fellow inmate to retract the original statement. She went on to say:

> I know this is devious, but it's the way I think. I would make him think it was all about him and me. In the meantime, do what these ladies are saying, get yourself a reliable residence, get a job, go to a treatment program and parenting workshops (if asked) and document the times you go. Before you know it, you'll have those kids."

Several other women cautioned her to keep the "system" out of her business and seek her family's assistance.

Whereas I relied on what I knew and did not have the confidence to believe that I could work a man this way, this woman did. Her approach was commonsense, while the one employed by Gina and me was more theoretical in nature. Theoretically, if the woman who asked the question followed the directives of the courts and social service agencies, she would be granted custody of her children. Realistically, the responses given by Gina and I (both people of color) expressed relative faith in the courts and tacitly acknowledged a belief that they are fair. As I reflected upon my answer, I pondered my naiveté. Academically, I know that the courts and social service agencies do not, frequently, serve the best interests of people of color and the poor, so why did I reply in such a fashion? Did I mentally note that the woman asking the question was White and that these systems might work differently for her? Did my limited knowledge of criminal justice systems and bureaucracies translate into an inability to view them from the perspective of those disempowered by them?

As I continued to reflect, I came to accept that my response was based on my privileged view as an outsider to such bureaucratic entities. Thus, my socioeconomic status distanced me from the women inmates in this instance.

It remains my belief that, through the study, the women will be able to make positive contributions to the studies of literacy, especially women's uses of it, and Black epistemology. As a researcher, I believe that my distinctive "outsider-within" status has and will continue to enhance my ability to understand and interpret their stories. Collins (1990) describes "outsider-within" status as uniquely ascribed to Black Womanist researchers. The position affords one the ability to understand the ramifications of one's research for the mainstream. Yet, such status also brings discernment regarding the marginality and injustice experienced and related by other Black women, who are also one's research participants.

I am not naive enough to believe that I will understand *all* that the women will share. As evidenced in the exchange regarding the Black woman who advised the woman presenting the threat, I realize that while the women and me share race and gender, we are dissimilar in significant ways (e.g., socioeconomic status and educational attainment). Thus, it is clear that "I will never [truly] know the experience of others, but I can know my own, and I can approximate theirs by entering their world {through} . . . social research" (Reinharz as quoted in Belenky, Clinchy, Goldberger and Tarule, 1986, 113).

At this point in time, I await a response as to whether I will be able to continue my work with the women of the Bergen County Jail, involving them in a research project of this scale. I began work in July and I proposed a continuation of the project in August. It is now the middle of March and I am uncertain as to when (or if) I will receive clearance from the Bergen County Sheriff's office to carry through. As there are a myriad of plausible reasons for the delay, I will not speculate. I will state, however, that I am aware that the political nature of the research might generate concern for both, those within and outside of the academy.

In documenting the genesis and initiation of this project (via this essay), I have attempted to chart the development of my own research interests as intimately connected with issues of identity and community, as well as in full alignment with the tenets of Womanist scholarship.

Whose Interests Are Served in Research With Black Research Participants?

Even in the initiation of such research (as described above), I have faced several battles. The most prominent, and the one on which I will focus for the remainder of the essay, centers on the type of research proposed.

The research approach that I suggest is qualitative, as I propose to gather data through the use of multiple interviews. Further, the findings extrapolated will be subject to my own interpretations as they are negotiated with the women with whom I will work. Thus, there is little pretense. My findings are highly subjective and colored by the manner in which I perceive and interpret the data collected.

In the mere proposal of such research, there will be those who counter it with the charge that culturally syncretized researchers (those who share similar cultural backgrounds with their research participants) cannot be objective "in their analyses of those problems which are so close to their life experiences" (Reyes and Halcon 1996, 97). It is odd that this same criticism is not leveled at White researchers who conduct research with White research participants (Smitherman 1988). In fact, it appears that White researchers frequently have the fewest restrictions placed on them. They routinely receive the opportunities to study their own and become expert on us, as well. Thus, it appears that the artificial contrivance of objectivity becomes just another tool with which to devalue the work of those whose mere presence within the academy creates disequilibrium.

The qualitative and subjective research approach that I have described is compatible with my philosophical orientation to research; an orientation that acknowledges the paradigmatic and social constructionist nature of research (Freydberg 1993; Vaz 1993). "It has been fairly well documented that knowledge is socially constructed and that the scholar's position influences what he/she recognizes as 'knowledge,' 'truth,' or 'science'" (Smitherman 1988, 146). Paradigmatic research and social constructionism acknowledge the absence of true objectivity or empirical derivation. Instead, "scientific facts are viewed as values, passing as answers for questions by individuals with definite political interests' (Vaz 1993, 87).

This research approach is also reflective of my view of scholarship and the tradition of Womanist epistemology which centers on a "dialectic of oppression and activism" (Collins 1990, 5). I privilege a "passionate scholarship, science-making [which is] rooted in, animated by and expressive of our values" (DuBois as quoted in Belenky et al. 1986, 141). "[T]he myth of dispassionate investigation bolsters the epistemic authority of white men," resulting in their "emotional hegemony" (Jagger as quoted in Wallace 1990, 54).

I also readily accept that Black women's epistemology (knowledge construction) is focused on examining the everyday thoughts and ideas of

Black women not previously identified as Black female intellectuals; it deconstructs the false distinction between thinking and living (doing); it privileges our collective legacy of struggle and survival (Collins, 1990).

In giving primacy to a Womanist form of scholarship, I think about the role that Black female intellectuals have historically undertaken. I reflect upon the scholarship of Black women, many of whom have seemingly understood and rejected traditional approaches to research and scholarship because of the mainstream interests potentially served by them. The work of Ida Wells-Barnett and her mobilization of the antilynching crusade comes to mind, as well as the manner in which her life experience was intricately linked to her scholarship. I also think of Mary Church Terrell, the Club Movement, and the way in which scholarship/activism prompted social change. From early in our history in the United States, Black women scholars have intricately linked "doing" and the reinforcement of cultural values and connection (Gordon 1995; Collins 1990; Davis 1981).

Empathy, an ethic of care, commitment to political praxis and reconstructist social change are intimately tied to Black epistemology and Black scholarship generally, as they are for many scholars from other traditionally marginalized groups and feminist scholars. In *Caring: A Feminine Approach to Ethics and Moral Education* (1984), Nel Noddings describes the links between the three:

> Apprehending one's reality, feeling what he feels as nearly as possible, is the essential part of caring from the view of the one-caring. For if I take on the other's reality as possibility and begin to feel its reality, I feel, also, that I must act accordingly; that is, I am impelled to act as though in my own behalf, but in behalf of the other . . . I must make a commitment to act (16).

For many Black male scholars, there has, traditionally, been more emphasis on balancing their research interests with those of the mainstream (e.g., E. Franklin Frazier, Charles Johnson). Although evidence suggests that the trend is apparently dissipating with a new generation of Black male scholars like William Cross, Michael Eric Dyson, John Hope Franklin, Robin Kelly, Manning Marable, and Cornel West.

Historically, while many Black male scholars have felt the altruistic need to demonstrate caring and commitment to the Black community, they have concomitantly been faced with meeting external and contrived demands for a nonexistent objectivity and empirical derivation (Banks 1992). I believe that this schizophrenic struggle is based on the longer and more secure tenure that Black men have experienced within the academy (in relation to Black women); so this need for balance was essential for survival.

Further, their efforts to pursue research in an objective fashion were largely based on their desire to secure legitimacy in academia, an institution that has had a long-held tradition of denying the intellectual capacity of people of color and women (Banks 1992; Franklin 1989).

Yet, pockets of Black male scholars have always resisted and remonstrated against such research demands and considered the implications of Black scholarship for the Black masses. I think of the young radical Black intelligentsia of the early 1900s, who collectively articulated the counter-hegemonic position that the Black educational elite might serve to actually benefit the black masses (Gordon 1990; Anderson 1978). I think of the sophisticated and brilliant scholarship of W.E.B. DuBois and Carter G. Woodson, and their advancement of research which was both culturally relevant and transformational.

I have been led to more fully question the utility of the historically privileged scientific paradigm that has driven much of academic research. In the guise of science, enslaved Black women have been used as racial guinea pigs in the perfection of complex gynecological surgeries (Breggin and Breggin 1998; Scully 1980). Poor, Black women have been exploited for the purpose of testing experimental and damaging birth control devices (Corea 1977). In addition, within the parameters of the Tuskegee Experiment, Black families were forced to suffer the effects of syphilis without the benefit of relief. I was nonplused by the HBO movie "Miss Evers' Boys" (based upon the experiment) and the creative choice to focus upon the complicity of the Black nurse, Miss Evers, rather than the government's blatant disregard for the male research subjects and their families (that could also be interpreted as racial animus).

Patently racist theories of biological determinism and eugenics have been advanced and gained credibility through the use of positivist philosophical orientations and empirical methodology (Breggin and Breggin 1998; Gould 1996; Steinem 1992; Davis 1981). Traditionally, research conducted within the confines of the academy and focused on people of color has advanced theories of racially derived pathology and the perpetuation of stereotypical, unidimensional portraits.

While I would not make the essentialist claims that all White researchers conduct this type of research or all researchers of color and feminists approach their research participants with honorable intentions, I would state that, more consistently, researchers from traditionally marginalized cultures study their communities in a more empathic and culturally sensitive fashion.

Chapter 5

Toward Self-Definition of Black Maternal Epistemology

My approach to day-care selection for my two-year-old daughter defied my academic training and makes me ashamed, retrospectively. In between work and worry about intensifying fatigue and malaise, I attempted to select a suitable day-care program. Without adequately comprehending the tenuous nuances that make contemporary day-care searches comparable to those for four-year colleges, I commenced the inquiry in April. The anticipation was that Z. would begin in September. Lamentably, I had no organized plan that would facilitate the exploration and only a theoretical notion of an appropriate site.

Within a brief duration, I located a site that I found appealing. I awaited communication from the center's directors as we attempted to coordinate the days my daughter attended with those I taught. In late August, I had not received the necessary advisement. Hastily, I decided to place my daughter in a setting that didn't possess a number of the desired features. Only minimal consolation was secured in its close proximity to my home, church-sponsorship, and adequate educational plan. Family friends reassured me of the facility's suitability and expressed satisfaction with their daughter's progress. Mentally, I noted that their observations were made without the benefit of training in education.

So, starting the second week in September, my child attended the second-choice daycare site. Though I was not ecstatic about it, my most pressing concerns centered on my eminent return to work and my sister's return to day classes during the Fall semester. My sister had cared for my daughter since she was a newborn.

The first day I dropped Z. off, I noticed that none of the teachers in a large area resembling a gymnasium acknowledged her presence or mine. She looked up at me, with uncertainty in her eyes, and I ignored it.

Though somewhat dismayed, I attributed the slight to the staff being exceptionally busy. The observation was mentally recorded. Subsequently, I asked my sister to pay close attention when she picked Z. up that afternoon. When I arrived home after a late evening class, my sister shook her head and announced (in a customarily understated fashion), "I found Z. wandering alone and it wasn't good."

The next day, my mother and I picked Z. up. We walked throughout the entire site, without presenting ourselves to the staff or once being asked for identification. We reached the back exit (near the director's office) without a word leveled at us. In this vicinity, my daughter and a young friend wandered, without their shoes. Their pull-up diapers obviously hadn't been changed nor had anyone attempted to toilet them. The school's administrator sat in her office, staring into space. My gaze averted to the face of my child. She looked disoriented and wild. Tears welled in her eyes and fury rose in mine. Forthwith, I approached the director and inquired about the state in which I found my daughter. Her responses I deemed unsatisfactory.

So, we gathered Z.'s belongings and went home. My mother took my daughter upstairs for a snack and bath. I remained on the stairs and wept. After composing myself, I returned to the school to inform the director that Z. would not return and reiterate my reasons for disenrollment. During the course of the next week, my daughter was enrolled in the site that had been my first choice. Though there are small problems that occasionally arise in the new setting, the staff and my family work in educational partnership. We are committed to Z.'s best interests.

Until the day that I found my daughter in the condition described, I didn't know that my heart could ache so intensely for someone other than myself. Pregnant and sick on those stairs, tears rolled down my face in spite of efforts to control them. Truthfully, the fact that I was pregnant again and expecting a baby, when I hadn't even mastered mothering the first, possibly exacerbated the flow of tears. But, it was not the primary reason for them.

Emphasizing the Hope in Hopelessness?

On those steps, I felt the ambivalent emotions of despair and joy, a joy that came from the recognition of my intense love for my child. The despair was attached to the fact that my own ineptitude as a mother had surfaced once again and prompted sobbing on one level. Once again, I had not met my own expectations as a mother. I was propelled back to days immediately following Z.'s birth—days during which I hadn't been able to detect that breastfeeding wasn't nourishing her. While I observed and related that she was very fussy and uncomfortable, I didn't know that she was ill. I thank God for Z.'s pediatrician, her vigilance and ability to identify my baby's dehydration.

I cried as I stood in front of my daughter's incubator, holding her very tiny hand. But, I wasn't certain whether I cried for her or myself, because the challenge mothering posed was too great. After all, shouldn't my maternal instinct have proven operational? If it had, my baby would be healthy. Shouldn't I have known, instinctually, that my child was not thriving?

Years later, I would watch young mother Tabitha Waldron (a young woman, in the Bronx, who had been tried and convicted for starving her baby to death). As Waldron appeared on varied, televised newsmagazines and the local news broadcasts, she explained that a prior breast reduction had obviously stopped the milk flow in her breasts. Further, she stated that she was unaware that the condition existed as she breastfed her baby; she didn't know that the baby was not being nourished. Waldron also contended that she had taken her child to a local clinic or hospital, only to be turned away because she didn't have a valid Medicaid card. Medicaid is a social welfare program, instituted in 1965, to defray medical and health costs for those receiving public assistance.

One newsmagazine program, in particular, juxtaposed Waldron's image with White, middle class mothers who had similar experiences, only they had not been tried for killing their babies.

Thoughts of my experience plagued me once more. As local news broadcasts offered damning court photographs of a withered, discolored baby and the incriminating testimony of the baby's father (who was portrayed as a frequent visitor to Waldron's home), my thoughts focused on my own inability to detect a similar health crisis for my baby, in spite of a doctorate and thirteen years' more life experience than Waldron. Yet, there remained a few glaring distinctions between the young mother and me. Primarily, her baby was dead and mine alive. She was on trial for her baby's death. My socioeconomic status afforded my child health care that had been denied Ms. Waldron's baby.

Additionally, I wept as I thought about long hours at work during Z.'s infancy. Disproving colleagues' plausible notions that I had lost my edge or that my drive and ambition had softened as a result of motherhood outweighed my concerns for becoming a mother to my daughter. But, I also remained at work because it was the one arena in which I felt competent. As I had three unexpected, major surgeries and returned to work (all within four months of Z.'s birth), my sister and mother cared for her primarily. Instinctively, my sister seemed to know just the right way to care for my daughter. I did not. If Z. was hurt or became frightened, she reached for my sister rather than me.

A False Distinction . . . Good and Bad Mothers

In reiteration, however, I also felt exuberance that day. "It is difficult when writing about motherhood—or experiencing it—to be balanced about both its grim and satisfying aspects," (Ruddick 1980, 345).

The day became symbolic. It represented the first during which I truly felt like a mother or even recognized that there was a conceptual framework upon which motherhood was positioned. "What understanding begins to do is make knowledge available for use, and that's the urgency, that's the push, that's the drive" (Lorde 1984, 108–109).

Prior to motherhood and in a societally conditioned response, I would reply, when asked, that I wanted children. Yet, I never really anticipated their arrival. While I recognize that there are many women who plan and prepare for motherhood, there are a number of us who fall into it in the fashion that I have described. Unexpectedly, I found myself pregnant twice. Though I readily support other women's right to abortion, I have found it an unacceptable option in my life. Motherhood came upon me by surprise and I was not ready for it.

Before motherhood, I had created a false dichotomy in respect to mothers. It is easy to idealize motherhood when one isn't caught up in the day-to-day realities of it. There were good mothers (those who sacrificed all) and bad mothers (those who made very little personal sacrifice). Quite naturally, my mother and maternal grandmother could be categorized as good mothers.

My mother loves learning and she is a dedicated teacher. Occasionally, she wistfully described the material possessions she might have had and the career choices that might have been available. Though she never mentioned it and I inadvertently discovered the information, I always thought that her decision to keep me rather than abort as my father had wished prevented her from attaining true happiness. In fact, he left and refused to marry her after the announcement of her decision. Eventually, he returned and they married for a brief period. I frequently reflect on her efforts to make life comfortable for my sister and me with little money and a great deal of self-sacrifice.

My maternal grandmother (Nana) reads voraciously, even as she has approached eighty. She has always loved words and remained enthralled by politics. But, she was unable to finish college, in spite of putting three children through college and graduate school. Though she has never complained or described her life choices with regret, she would have completed college (at least) if not for the encumbrances of domesticity, marriage, and motherhood. I had no reason to believe that I could willingly make such sacrifices and remain committed to creative production and intellectual pursuits. I worried about motherhood's potential impact on my creativity and my writing.

Yet, the most vivid portrait I had of a woman who chose art over motherhood was Camille Billops. Billops, a Black woman artist, worked in the visual arts, and made the decision to place her four-year-old daughter in an orphanage, in spite of the protests of her immediate family and their offers to raise the child, as Billops believed that mothering interfered with her production of art.

One night, my husband (at that time) and I looked at *Finding Christa*, a documentary film that chronicles Billops' relinquishment of parental rights, and her adult daughter's quest to reunite with her. At one point in the film, Billops' grown daughter attempts to hug her. She backs away, stating that she isn't ready for such a display. My ex seethed at this clip in particular. I viewed the complete story with great interest. He got up from his seat and began ranting and calling Billops every form of "bitch" and "lesbian" that came to his mind. I understood her struggle and came to her defense.

In a myriad of ways, I could relate to Billops. As I recounted the extraordinary film to women in my family and female colleagues, many of them showed visible signs of disgust and classified Billops as a bad mother. I felt as if they were speaking about me because I saw a clear reflection of myself in her. I clearly understood her commitment to art's creation. I could relate to her desire to produce art primarily, with all other responsibilities considered secondary. After all, very few criticize male artists for relinquishing their responsibilities as parents for art's sake. I am not saying that this model is one to emulate; instead I am speaking about the pervasiveness of it.

Stuck in a pattern of binary thought at that point, I felt compelled to accept the possibility that I might become a bad mother, like Billops . . . ultimately, sitting alone with my art, feathers in my braids and too much eye make-up.

My thoughts that I was en route to "bad mothering" were confirmed as I read Tillie Olsen's *Silences*, in which the author described motherhood as a possible halting of the creative process and cessation to writing. I shuddered as I listened to Toni Morrison describing her efforts to accommodate writing as her children slept. I was both intrigued and revolted as she related, in an interview, that her young son had vomited on her writing, she wiped the vomit away with her hand, and kept writing so she wouldn't forget the thought.

My fears and anxieties that motherhood served as an impediment to continued artistic production became self-fulfilling prophecies after Z.'s birth. For months, I was unable to write. I wrote feelings that I had not actualized, I wrote shit. In rereading, I knew the work was merely adequate. It was far from that which I considered my best. The pieces I submitted were frequently rejected and I, tacitly, understood the reasons.

Writing had always proven pleasurable. It had always worked as a type of release. Even the process of revision was engaging, though (in my view) it greatly resembles pregnancy and childbirth in its tedious and painstaking nature, but glorious product. Yet, at that time, I did not know if I would ever write again.

With time and reflection, I have come to accept that there is no ideal in respect to mothering. There is no fixed model of maternal perfection or imperfection. Instead, mothers (not only defined as those who physically give birth) are in states of flux, continuous processes of development. "The passions of maternity are so sudden, intense, and confusing that we ourselves often remain ignorant of the perspective, the thought that has developed from our mothering" (Ruddick 1980, 342).

Slowly, I am evolving into a mother and coming to the realization that working toward good parenting (as defined by my own criteria) is probably one of the most significant things I have ever done in life. I have grown to appreciate my daughter's hugs, kisses, and pronouncements that she wants to be "a sexy squirrel" when she grows up. I relish my one-year-old son's very wet kisses and giggles as he turns the VCR on and off while the family attempts to watch some program.

My children have definitely added to my life and made me a better person. Yet, getting to this point is an ongoing struggle. With the passage of time, I am learning from those mothers who have gone before me. There is tremendous comfort in the thought that "mothers, despite the inevitable trials and social conditions of motherhood, are often effective in their work" (Ruddick 1980, 344). While there are noteworthy lessons that I have learned from my own mother and grandmother, I continue to learn lessons in courage and survival like those told in essays by Toni Cade Bambara (1996), Nikki Giovanni (1988) Audre Lorde (1984), Jill Nelson (1997), among others. My experiences and feelings are validated as I read Alice Walker (1983) or revisit my thoughts about that Toni Morrison's interview and the realization that she wasn't complaining. I learn from the resourcefulness and organizational skills demonstrated by scholar Catherine Dorsey-Gaines (as she related them over lunch) or in Buchi Emcheta's writing process that began at 4 A.M. as her young children slept.

I am learning to ask for help when I need it because I can't do it alone. I am learning to write during odd hours as my children sleep or write book notes as my son looks on from his playpen and my daughter sits next to me with a book, asking every two minutes, "Are you finished writing yet? Are you ready to read?"

There are times when I simply can't go to the word processor because one child or the other isn't feeling well or needs me, so I write a code word or a phrase and return to it when life has returned to normal. As one of the characters in the movie *Down in the Delta* stated as she cared for an Alzheimer's patient, "You've got to learn to go with the craziness . . . don't fight it." I am learning just that.

Yet, my children have provided me with another gift of immeasurable worth. They have provided me with a new epistemological framework from which to work and prompted me to explore the concept of Black maternal epistemology and add to the body of extant knowledge which defines it.

> Raising Black children—female and male—in the mouth of a racist, sexist, suicidal dragon is perilous and chancy. If they cannot love and resist at the same time, they will probably not survive. And in order to survive, they must let go. This is what mothers teach—love, survival—that is self-definition and letting go (Lorde 1984, 74).

Defining Maternal Epistemology

Maternal epistemology, as defined by Ruddick (1980), encompasses "the intellectual capacities [the mother] develops, the judgments she makes, the metaphysical attitudes she assumes, the values she affirms" (347). "The discipline of maternal thought consists in establishing criteria for determining failure and success, in setting the priorities, and in identifying the virtues and liabilities which the criteria presume" (Ruddick 1980, 347).

Maternal epistemology is a concrete example of lived thought; an example of daily engagement in critical thought. Maternal epistemology can be legitimately defined as critical thought if the principles established by Matthew Lipman (1988) are considered. Lipman describes the outcomes of critical thinking as judgments and identifies them as reliant on criteria and displaying sensitivity to context. Maternal thought involves all three.

Ruddick raises another point in reference to maternal epistemology as she describes the paradox of power and powerlessness that motherhood presents. "Central to the experience of our mothers and our mothering is a poignant conjunction of power and powerlessness" (Ruddick 1980, 343). My thoughts immediately went to our mother ancestors (the enslaved) as they bore children without any rights to them. I am compelled by the ambivalent emotions and thoughts they experienced, upon learning that they were pregnant or assuming care of a child. Yet, it is even more illuminating to think that, within such peril and uncertainty, they knew that "becoming a mother was the most important of life's transitions for slave women and that caring for young children would always be an important female responsibility" (White 1985, 118).

In modern-day society, the incredible enigma of power and powerlessness remains potent for Black mothers. While one might be led to ponder the immense power in our reproductive capabilities, awe in our ability to give and sustain life, one might also be forced to contemplate the powerless ways in which we might appear to our children. How might they see us as we work for wages that are still not reflective of our worth, battle some fathers so that they might play more significant roles and make child-support payments for the well-being of our children, or as we, Black women, appear on television as the butt of jokes (even on supposedly reality-based shows).

Advancement of the Call for Self-Definition

Ten years ago, Patricia Hill Collins (1990) advocated, "the need for Black feminists to honor our mothers' sacrifice by developing an Afrocentric feminist analysis of Black motherhood" (115). Today, I repeat her call, though there has been some progress in this respect. There are a number of such accounts written in genres other than essay and expository text. I call for more nonfiction accounts that privilege us as thinkers. Though it appears that we are widely accepted as writers of fiction and poetry, our positions as intellectuals who advance knowledge construction through nonfiction are more tenuous in nature.

Comparatively, in relation to other aspects of Black womanhood, Black female intellectuals haven't spent as much time working toward self-definition by documenting our struggles with motherhood and further conceptualizing a Black maternal knowledge-construction process.

White and Black male scholars (e.g., U. B. Phillips, Thomas Nelson Page, Patrick Moynihan, William Wells Brown, W.E.B. DuBois, George Washington Williams) have spent inordinate amounts of time shaping our image and documenting our perceived failures and successes. A number of White feminists have eliminated us from such discussions. Therefore, it becomes obvious that we need to describe the thought that goes into *being* a Black mother, the way in which being Black-identified impacts child-rearing. We need to explain that solidly grounded reasoning substantiates our decision making.

Glimpses of Black Maternal Epistemology

There is both thought and beauty in the soft admonishments "to behave or don't act up in here" of Black mothers, who consider themselves exceptional in no particular way, to their youngsters in stores and other public facilities. For within that chiding, there is the unspoken understanding that their children's misbehavior will be perceived as confirmation about the entire race rather than an individual indiscretion.

Cultural relativity also greatly impacts parenting, proposes anthropologist John Ogbu. For instance, Black mothers (of all stations in life) might value obedience more than creativity, for many realize that any diversion from that path could prove life-threatening. Historically, questioning authority could result in lynching and violence. Today, it often results in death at the hands of the police or those of one's own people (Paul 2000).

Conversely, a number of White mothers in suburban environments might value creativity and critical thinking in their children. They might encourage their children to question and challenge authority. They are not conditioned to believe that such behavior could have deadly consequences. Their world-view and experiences would be incongruent with such a belief, in most instances (Paul 2000).

Black maternal thought goes into decision making centered on mundane and routine tasks like selecting clothing for children to wear to school. Scholar Jacquelyn Mitchell (1996) describes her experiences with Black mothers of Head Start children. She recounts her bafflement as she noticed that, in spite of warnings that their children should wear old clothes as they would probably dirty them while playing and exploring, the children arrived on the first day of school "impeccably" attired. Mitchell states that the mothers' actions seemed "senseless" and she "questioned the logic of their behavior" (74). Eventually, Mitchell came to understand that the decision was based on the mothers' fears that White teachers would consider the children "unkempt and neglected and treat them as such; the teachers would doubly judge their children—by outward appearance and by their appearance as Black children" (74).

There is a knowledge-construction process involved as incarcerated Black mothers sometimes work diligently to find acceptable placements for their children during their imprisonment or make attempts to secure visitation so that the children's feelings of abandonment might slowly dissipate.

Thought is also advanced as professional Black mothers discuss their decision making as they balance the demands of home and professional spheres. Further, much could be learned from Black female artists who discuss and write about their efforts to effectively parent their children and sustain their creative lives/livelihoods.

We have so many lessons yet to learn about motherhood written from the perspective of Black mothers, from all stations in life. We need to explain our hopes, dreams, aspirations, and fears for our children, as well as for ourselves. We need to capture the struggles we experience each day to raise children in this society, with partners and without, as well as the fulfillment and pride that come from seeing children act in ways that were shaped by our love, our sharing, our wisdom.

Chapter 6

The Electronic Auction Block

While dressing for work, I routinely watch television to expedite the process. Inadvertently, I channel-surf until something strikes my attention. A number of academic colleagues look bewildered if I mention television or a specific televised program (that is not educational) in casual conversation. Yet, I am not ashamed and I make no apologies. I am a *Gen-Xer,* a term used to describe those of us born between the years 1961 and 1980, and television has always been a facet of my life. For me, television serves as nonprint text. Text (in its print and nonprint forms) assists us in the process of constructivism, the comprehension of social, economic, and political relationships, and the ways in which those linkages operate within our societal infrastructure (Aronowitz 1989; Christian-Smith 1997; Jewell 1993; Smith 1989; and Smitherman and van Dijk 1988).

But, on a particular day, a scabrous piece of racial pornography hit my television screen. Two obese Black women fought each other, as a "breath and britches" (as my mother calls such men) sat between them, with seeming amusement. The fight was sparked by the women "blowin' his spot up," revealing that he continued to have sex with them both, although he had denied the allegation to each respectively. At this taping, he supposedly acknowledged his indiscretions for the first time, much to the women's obvious chagrin.

Viewers could plainly catch glimpses of the women's cellulite-covered posteriors and flabby breasts, large and sagging, as the two engaged in combat. They fought until one stood almost nude. The other breathed heavily and waved her opponent's braided wig to the crowd as an indication of her victory. During the fight, they called each other varied forms of "bitch" and "stank ho." The audience laughed heartily at the women's quaint use of dialect and corpulent forms in varied states of undress. While obesity has been named a national health crisis in the United States among the general population, the image of the fat Black woman has traditionally proven comedic, in respect to American iconography (Jewell 1993).

In their midst stood Jerry Springer, feigning disbelief and incredulity. A modern-day auctioneer, he stood, profiting from the commodification of Black bodies.

Profit Is the Primary Value Taught Via Television

Though I am routinely disgusted by that which I see on television, I am seldom surprised. Humanitarian concerns have been and remain of secondary importance for television executives. While "some news professionals believe . . . profitability should be secondary to educating the public for the common good, . . . news professionals aren't as powerful as accountants" (Postman and Powers 1992, 6).

Television programming, in all of its varied forms, is designed to generate profit. "The whole point of television is to get you to watch so that programmers, performers and others can rake in money" (Postman and Powers 1992, 3). Television's content is shaped to attract viewers and advertisers; thus, the more controversy generated by a show, the better. Advertisers see the equation in the following fashion: more viewers mean more potential customers.

Talk shows, like *Jerry Springer*, serve as "pseudo-news," "television's version of 'yellow journalism'," and an extended newspaper feature story in video format (Postman and Powers 1992, 92). Through the vehicle of the talk show, Jerry Springer fulfills a service and that service helps him to remain on television, in spite of some public outcry about the vile nature of his show and guests. In a similar fashion, Springer's self-identification as Jewish is far from coincidental. In the process of capitalizing on the inequities of race, gender, sexual orientation, and class as they play themselves out in the lives of his guests, he also allows himself to be used as an instrument in the reinforcement of the most aberrant stereotypes of Jews. The phenomenon of the talk show host's racial/ethnic and/or cultural affinities and accompanying stereotypes acting as marketable features has also been witnessed in other talk shows.

Yet, Springer serves another purpose as well. He helps to anesthetize American audiences by relegating blatant racism, sexism, other forms of intolerance, and obvious exploitation to positions of past excesses—social ills that we, as a nation, have overcome. After all, the reasons that Springer's guests entertain us have nothing to do with their disenfranchisement and powerlessness. And, isn't there something slightly perverse about being entertained by the pain and devastation experienced by others?

Many are able to view *The Jerry Springer Show* as an aberration; an immoderation; as such, the blatant racism and discrimination set forth is accepted, within that context. In a similar manner, many are only able to see discrimination and hate in their most extreme forms like the dragging death of James Byrd in Texas, the beating death of Matthew Shepard in the Midwest, or the police assassinations of Eleanor Bumpurs and Amadou Diallo.

Via his "guests," Springer confirms for audiences that the majority of poor Blacks, Latinos, and Whites remain disadvantaged because of their own ignorance, deviant behavior, and lack of personal responsibility. Typically, the privileged have utilized images as ways in which to substantiate the contention that certain groups in society have limited resources and power because of flaws inherent in themselves or in the cultures to which they ascribe (Jewell 1993). Thus, there is no impetus for change or need for the privileged to divest from maintenance of the status quo.

Even if one chooses against criticizing the guests because of the predicaments in which they find themselves, the criticism might simply rest on the fact that they were "stupid enough" to appear on the show at all. I routinely hear those who watch Springer justify their viewing with the contention that the show's guests collude in their own exploitation. After all, they know what they're getting into. Yet, in a society in which some have so little, a plane ticket, an overnight hotel stay, and fifteen minutes of questionable fame might prove irresistible enticements.

The more times during which we are able to see these images of the disenfranchised as aberrant and perverse, the more easily accepted they are. I do not contend that the images presented on television act on us, unfiltered, and I recognize that all viewers (readers of text) interpret the messages they read differently (Paul 1999). Yet, the bombardment of anomalous images of Blacks, Latinos, gays, the indigent, and the disabled in reality-based television programming firmly implants those representations in the American psyche and further advances institutionalized racism and other forms of discrimination (Paul 1999; Jewell 1993; Turner 1994).

Another tragic outcome of such negative images is that they affect the racial self-concepts and identities of those from traditionally marginalized cultures. The viewing of these images has consequential outcomes on the individual and collective psyche of colonized people. We begin to believe and accept that which is presented about us (Paul 1999; hooks 1994a; Jewell 1993; Turner 1994).

Black women on *The Jerry Springer Show* are made to appear like bitches, "ho's" and other images from a "Shahrazad Ali nightmare" (Wallace 1992, 124), even though it is equally important to acknowledge that Black women on the show (like other disempowered groups that appear) frequently collude in their own exploitation. Ali, a Black woman, wrote the infamous *The Blackman's Guide to Understanding the Blackwoman* (1989). In the book, the author provides Black men with insights about Black women that should facilitate their understanding of us. Her insights include equating us with "wild savage boars," "rat{s} who behave like dog{s} while purring like cat{s}" and encouraging Black men to "soundly slap {us} in the mouth." It is further noted that "despite Ali's insistence that the book was 'the culmination of many years of study, observation and research,' it was almost impossible to deduce what her sources were from reading it" (Wallace 1992, 124). Unfortunately some of these images presented by Ali can be manipulatively substantiated as one sees us "actin' a fool" on The *Jerry Springer Show.*

Links in the Commodification of Black Bodies

Historically, Black women's bodies have been used as freak show oddities for the pleasure of White masses. As I viewed the spectacle presented via Springer, I was propelled back in time to the 1810 exhibition of Saartjie Baartman, a.k.a. Sarah Bartman, Saat-Jee, or the Hottentot Venus. I imagined the humiliation she probably felt as her buttocks (the major attraction) were manipulated for the crowd's gratification. Saddest of all, I thought of the postmortem removal of Saartjie's genitalia and buttocks and their placement on display (in Paris' Musee de l'Homme) as the ultimate indignity.

Contemplation led me to the ways in which imagery has been used as justification in the continued abuse and misuse of Black women. Stereotypes have been used to mitigate the potency of oppression and domination, vindicating social inequity.

For example, Black enslaved women were sometimes described by professional historians as "clumsy, awkward, gross, elephantine . . . pouting, grinning, leering . . . sensual and shameless" (Hart 1906, 93, 98).

In the name of nineteenth-century science, images of the Black woman as possessing a "lascivious, apelike sexual appetite . . . [that led us] to copulate with apes" (Gilman 1985, 213) were advanced. Through medical literature citations from the same time period, allegations were made that the overdevelopment of Black female genitalia heightened our propensity for lascivity. Thus, a number of slaveholders were able to justify their rape of slave women by emphasizing Black women's insatiable sexual appetites (Morton 1991; Davis 1981).

Further, these images helped to bolster the traditional and symbolic juxtaposition of Black and White female bodies; a juxtaposition reliant upon Black bodies as the antithesis of the demure sensuality, femininity, and aestheticism represented by the icon of the White female body. Instead, the Black female body, iconoclastically representative of a raw, Black female sexuality, proves abnormal, utilitarian, and distorted.

This false, yet accepted, distinction of womanhood and femininity also propped up miscegenation laws and the "necessity" of lynching. After all, White female chastity was at stake; even so, Ida Wells-Barnett successfully used White journalists' own accounts to invalidate this premise and expose lynching as a tool used to reinforce and maintain the political and economic subordination of Black men (Davis 1981; Carby 1985).

Today, such images are used in a similar fashion, although, in most forms, they are more subtle in nature.

The New Racism

In contemporary society, race (when used by the mainstream) "has become metaphorical—a way of referring to and disguising forces, events, classes, and expressions of social decay and economic division far more threatening to the body politic than biological 'race' ever was" (Morrison 1992, 63).

In her illuminating *Playing in the Dark: Whiteness and the Leterary Imagination* (1992), Morrison states that Blackness has, historically, been used as a gauge against which Whiteness was calibrated and celebrated, even when Blackness was not mentioned. The absence of Blackness proves as powerful in defining the concept of Whiteness as its presence.

In today's society, this concept is further advanced. Yet, an interesting twist has been added. There are now code words that signify Blackness, even though Blackness itself remains unmentioned. For example, "welfare," "Affirmative Action," "quotas rather than excellence," "angry," "criminal," and "homeless" all seem to equate with Blackness in the contemporary American psyche. Images, such as a number of those presented on news and reality-based programming, remain fixed in the minds of politicians and their constituencies as they institute insouciant policy initiatives.

For example, a 1997 Yale University study (conducted by Martin Gilens) suggested that the news media used photographs and other visual representations of Blacks more frequently than those of Whites to illustrate stories about poverty, even though the majority of the poor continue to be White. In a five-year examination of magazine articles and television newscasts, Gilens determined that national news magazines, including *Time, Newsweek,* and *U.S. News & World Report,* pictured Blacks sixty-two percent of the time in stories on poverty. Televised, evening news broadcasts juxtaposed Black images with poverty sixty-five percent of the time.

There have been countless instances in which the Black image has been used to evoke a groundswell, impacting public opinion. We can think back to the way in which the face of Willie Horton, equated with recidivists who are let out of jail to murder innocent White folk, was brilliantly paired with that of Michael Dukakis (by the Bush war room) and effectively cost Dukakis the 1988 presidential election.

Many of us remember the way in which the nation galvanized in support of Susan Smith whose children were stolen by an unidentified Black man, only to discover that Smith had killed her own children. It wasn't so long ago that a technically darkened photograph of O.J. Simpson appeared on the cover of *Newsweek* at the time of his booking. If O.J. is a murderer, isn't he one in spite of skin hue? In too many instances, it appears as if the most effective route to capturing a suspect and instilling pervasive fear remains the Blackening of the suspect.

Text and talk constitute the social and political dimensions of structural racism in present-day society (Smitherman and van Dijk 1988, 12). In this sense, "talk and text not only may hurt you, they also may hurt you more effectively, more systematically, and more permanently" (Smitherman and van Dijk 1988, 11). Talk, text, and the presentation of racialized images impact public policy. "The mass media help focus our attention on specific problems and public policy issues, that is, set the public agenda" (Daniel and Allen 1988, 25).

For me, this point of image was driven home, most forcefully, within the last month here in the tristate area of New York, New Jersey, and Connecticut. During this time span, a young female, out-of-towner, Nicole Barrett, was hit with a brick by an unidentified "Black, homeless man." A sketch of the assailant was posted in the various city-based newspapers and all the local televised news broadcasts. This posting occurred within a week of Mayor Rudolph Guiliani's controversial announcement that homeless people staying in public shelters would be required to work during the day in order to remain in shelters at night. There have also been proposals that the children of homeless families be removed and placed within a less-than-stellar New York City foster care system.

Three days after the brick assault and sketch posting of a clearly Black, male face, the NYPD commenced to crack down on homeless people. Forty-four homeless people were arrested in a day. That number represented the largest bust of homeless people in a single day, according to a news story in *The New York Post*, 25 November 1999. During 1998, there were a total of 242 homeless arrested for the entire year.

Police officials justified the arrests with confirmation that officers had been instructed to offer help and ask the homeless to move, prior to arresting them. Yet, as echoed by attorney Norman Siegel of the New York Civil Liberties Union, "Since when has sleeping on the streets become a crime?"

Ultimately, 36-year-old Paris Drake (identified as a recidivist) was charged with the attack. Facts that were not readily available included those which stated that, although he had been on the streets for a short period at a particular point, Drake was not homeless nor was he deranged. He was crack addicted. Some accounts state that Drake hit Ms. Barrett with the brick accidentally as he aimed at an accomplice. Finally, the NYPD had Drake in custody a day or two after the attack on a different charge, yet released him, unaware that he was a suspect in the alleged brick attack.

The Black face of Paris Drake helped to accelerate the institution of policies that adversely impact the homeless and exhibit racism and sexism. Fortunately, however, people in the tristate area, across positionalities, have seen the policies for what they are and they have taken to the streets in protest, even proposing to sleep on the steps of City Hall.

The new racism is, generally, "indirect and only subtly physical, as with social policies that directly affect minority life. Language and discourse are vital in this reproducing of racial oppression and control of blacks and other minorities" (Smitherman and van Dijk 1988, 17).

Chapter 7

Rap and Orality: Critical Media Literacy, Pedagogy, and the Issue of Cultural Synchronization

As I sit, engaged in composing this text on the struggles of urban center teachers to provide their students with culturally relevant pedagogical practices, two popular culture muses, Louanne Johnson (of the 1995 biopic *Dangerous Minds*) and Bill Rago of the 1996 movie *Renaissance Man*) guide me. The image of Louanne's (Michelle Pfeiffer) determined face comes to mind, as she strives to make the high school English curriculum meaningful and her initial efforts to conjugate verbs with students fail. As only movie magic would have it, the viewer sees Louanne's students reach epiphany as they connect the Bob Dylan songs that they have probed in class with the poems of Dylan Thomas.

In a similar scenario, instructor Bill Rago (Danny DeVito) takes his class, a group of six urban center and two rural Army recruits (dubbed as the "Double D's"—Dumb as Dog Shit), from barely expressing interest in the complexity of Shakespeare's *Hamlet* to using the texts of their own lives to make connections to the play. Ultimately, Bill is rewarded for his painstaking efforts as his students "rap" the play's synopsis for him. Once again, within two hours, the viewer is able to witness students coming to the educational light. Please note that both popular culture teachers use aspects of students' perceived cultures to pedagogically lure them to work that can be considered canonical. Smith (1989) defines *pedagogical lures* as "come-ons offered by teachers to students reluctant or unwilling to appreciate the virtues of the canonical curriculum (33)."

The teacher-muses to which I have alluded keep a couple of thoughts central for me. One, for most teachers who work with urban center student populations, teaching is not so easy and students don't experience

contrived epiphanies. Secondly, the struggle to find appropriate, culturally relevant practices (that don't, concomitantly, degenerate to mere teaching lures) is rarely seamless, swift, or facile. Providing urban center, Black
and Latino youngsters (in secondary school) with literacy development
practices which advance critical thought necessitates great creativity, vi-
sionary thinking, and comprehension of cultural dynamics.

Urban center teachers, like many teachers nationwide, are faced with
the challenge of finding innovative, educationally sound approaches that
consider and develop the cultural capital that students bring to the classroom, as well as making education relevant and purposeful. Bourdieu (as
quoted in Finders 1997, 37) defines *cultural capital* as "the beliefs, cultural background, knowledge, and skills that are passed from one generation to the next."

The primary focus of this chapter is the use of rap in the classroom as
a site of critical inquiry. Within the context of this article, rap is distinguished from hip hop. Hip hop philosopher KRS-One characterizes hip
hop as "a consciousness"; a state of being. Rap is the music of hip hop. In
her book entitled *Black Noise: Rap Music and Black Culture in Contemporary America* (1994), scholar Tricia Rose distinguishes rap as one
of hip hop's three integral components. The other two are graffiti and
breakdancing.

Rap artist Q-Tip further demarcates in a song entitled "Check the
rime" by stating that "rap is not pop if you call it that then stop." This
point is elucidated when numerous comments about rap's controversy as
solely based upon its nature as a new, irreverent music, like rock and roll,
are considered. The synergy of race and class place rap on its own cultural terrain.

Rap can be viewed as firmly situated within the Afrodiasporic "oral,
poetic, and protest traditions to which it is clearly and substantially in-
debted" (Rose 1994, 25).

> Rap forebears stretch back through disco, street funk, radio DJs, Bo Diddley, the
> bebop singers, Cab Calloway, Pigmeat Markham, . . . tap dancers and comics,
> The Last Poets, Gil Scott Heron, Muhammad Ali, a cappella, and doo wop groups,
> ring games, skip rope rhymes, prison and army songs, toasts, signifying, and the
> dozens (Toop as quoted in Rose 1994, 85).

Rap's tradition can also be traced to "soul rapper Millie Jackson, the
classic Blues women . . . 'Blaxsploitation' films like Sweet Sweetback's
Baadass Song," Donald Goines' gangsta fiction, and 'pimp narratives,'"
(Rose 1994, 55).

The significance of the chapter lies in the premise that rap can privilege student voices, especially those of Black and Latino, urban center youth, while simultaneously teaching them to interrogate those voices (Giroux and Simon 1989; Giroux 1990). Rap can serve as a literature, independently, without necessarily being paired with other literatures. Rap can foster a "pedagogy which engages popular culture in order to affirm rather than mute the voice of the student" (Giroux and Simon 1989, 228).

While I am aware that there are students from other races and ethnicities present in urban centers across the nation and students from various cultures enjoy the cultural phenomenon of rap, I predominantly focus on Blacks and Latinos. The decision is based upon having the most experience, as a teacher, with these groups. Further, within the context of this chapter, I contend that these groups have been and remain consequentially disenfranchised, educationally, economically, and socially within the United States (Banks 1995, Darling-Hammond 1995, Crenshaw, Gotanda, Peller, and Thomas 1995, Marable 1996, and Guinier 1998).

During the course of the chapter, I will talk about those positionalities that led me to view rap as a valuable site of exploration. I will additionally review the way in which I initially used rap in a South Bronx classroom. Then, I will chart my attempts to introduce an instructional strategy focused on rap and critical interrogation to secondary school teachers; some of whom struggled in their efforts to enhance cultural synchronization within their respective classes.

The Issue of Cultural Synchronization

Culture, itself, is "emergent, contested, and consequently always in the process of being constructed, reconstructed as an historical production," (Carlson and Apple 1998, 1). Thus, culture plays an essential role in classrooms and schools, as it does in society at large. Cultural synchronization is a harmony established between the cultural systems of schools, diverse groups of learners, and the communities from which those learners come (Gay 1993; Irvine 1991). Further, it is maintained that present-day cultural manifestations (reflective of identifiable Black and/or Latino cultural norms, language, behaviors, and attitudes) are most prevalent in lower socioeconomic status communities "where racial isolation persists and assimilation into the majority culture is minimal" (Irvine 1991, 24). Thus, teachers who are cultural outsiders to the communities in which they work, many times misunderstand and misinterpret the cultural nuances present.

The process of developing an effective pedagogical repertoire is complicated by the lack of cultural synchronization shared between many teachers and their students, This lack of cultural continuity in classrooms can result in cultural misunderstanding, student resistance, low teacher expectation for student success, and self-fulfilling prophecies of student failure. Research findings indicate that student resistance was reinforced when "the teacher's primary emphasis was academic subject matter; and acceptance was more likely when students' personal knowledge was incorporated into instruction in conjunction with a responsive style of classroom discourse" (Mahiri 1998, 2; Alpert 1991).

Rap in a South Bronx Classroom

Upon entering the classroom as a novice teacher in the New York City public school system, I was confronted with intermediate school students who were not 'turned on' to school, for the most part. Yet, they did find great pleasure in popular culture art forms like computer games, television, rap audiotapes, and video (Glenn-Paul 1997). I grew up in the same community in which I taught and popular culture has been a significant aspect of my life as well. The television always served as background noise in my home. News was received via the community and televised broadcast, although my stepfather brought the *New York Times* home daily. Rhythm and blues played consistently. Black art and visual representations of Blackness were omnipresent. Rap was part of the world that I shared with my two best girlfriends and other contemporaries.

Primarily, I shared many of the same cultures to which my students belonged; thus, I tried to devise a way in which to mesh those cultural dimensions with literacy development. I had a perfect window of opportunity when I decided to introduce the genre of poetry. Many of my students seemed to bring limited knowledge of the topic to discussions. Through further discussion, exposure, cooperative learning groups, the modalities of sight, sound, and touch as well as the use of rap, students explored the substance of poetry.

Students sought to define poetry in art, song, greeting cards, motion, dance, and nursery rhymes (Glenn-Paul 1997). Further, they were engaged in activities which led them to explore poetry written in Spanish, although a number didn't understand the language. Together, they deciphered some basic qualities of poetry that existed, independent of potential language barriers.

We inquired, collaboratively, into the relationships between rap, the music of groups like Arrested Development, MC Serch, KRS-One, Public

Enemy, and A Tribe Called Quest and the poetry of Emily Dickinson, William Shakespeare, Edgar Allan Poe, Langston Hughes, Nikki Giovanni, and Gwendolyn Brooks.

I was extremely excited by my students' enthusiasm over their discoveries that rap was a valid poetic form. According to Purves (1993), "regardless of a poet's culture, that poet uses rhythm, imagery, typography, grammar and syntax as the medium of the poem" (358). Using the criteria cited, rap can be classified as poetry legitimately.

Positionality and the Use of Rap in Teacher Preparation

As I moved to the role of teacher educator, I started to introduce this culturally relevant, instructional strategy to the teachers with whom I worked. Undoubtedly, my younger students focused on their learnings about the content of the poems and the conceptualization of poetry generally; the teachers, however, focused on issues of disenfranchisement, power, and authority related to the lesson. Specifically, they wrote:

> Experienced what it is like to be in a learning situation where I did not understand what was going on. I didn't understand a word of the rap music (loved the beat . . .).

> The trouble for bilingual individuals in translating information was evident in our grp.[sic], since we received a poem in a foreign language. Techniques [such] as repetition, looking for familiar words, and the format of the writing was used in order to decode.

> The privilege and power of the language . . . these are points I never thought of before.

> Poetry can be defined as personal stories of injustice. The artform that is chosen by the poet should not be the determining factor as to whether or not it is poetry.

The exercise also led some of them, however, to confront me on consequential points. First of all, although I initially failed to acknowledge the criticism' validity, they contended that I was also accountable for using popular culture as a lure to move students toward more traditional literatures. They also confirmed that while I shared a number of cultural points of reference with my students (e.g., language, music, race, youth), they did not, necessarily, share those reference points.

The latter point is magnified when recent school demographic trends are taken into account. As the percentage of students of color within the U.S. public school system increases, the teaching force remains White and female. According to the National Center for Education Statistics

(NCES) (1993), one in three students currently enrolled in public elementary and secondary schools is from a traditionally marginalized group (e.g., Asian/Pacific Islander, Black, Latino, and Native American). The same statistical account (NCES 1993) reports that people of color compose only 13 percent of the teaching force. Women make up more than 70 percent of the teaching corp. Further, "whereas a growing percentage of students are poor and live in large, urban areas, increasing numbers of teachers are middle class and reside in small- to medium-size suburban communities" (Gay 1993).

Aside from race and socioeconomic status, age also proves a cultural barrier. Most teachers are middle-aged and many view contemporary youth culture as possessing qualities antithetical to those with which they were reared and rampant with a cynicism and smugness quite similar to that described in Nirvana's "Smells Like Teen Spirit," in which the verse "Here we are now, entertain us" reverberates. Contemporary youth come of age in a society that privileges market logic. The principle of consumption reigns supreme and the message is clearly and quickly dispensed: "I purchase, therefore I am" (McLaren and Gutierrez 1998, 308).

Also, today's youngsters live at a time in which they cannot take their physical security for granted, they must navigate the traps of gang violence, school violence, and AIDS. They commit suicide in record numbers (Mahiri, 1998).

For me, the sense of distance that teachers describe in their relationships with their teen-aged students is exacerbated as race and class are factored into the equation. For example, many urban center students and their respective communities privilege knowledge that is experiential and lived and they value popular culture art forms (hooks 1989; Giroux and Simon 1989; James 1993). Then they are thrust into school systems and encounter teachers who have often conveyed the sense that such knowledges and epistemologies are substandard and without value. This lack of valuation leads to my discussion of the second dilemma I faced. That dilemma centered on pragmatics.

The teachers with whom I worked stated that they were accustomed to teacher educators presenting abstract concepts without application. Instead, they wanted to discuss both the pragmatics of implementation as well as theory. Specifically, they posed questions and expressed concerns like:

> Is playing rap a means of saying, "But I do promote multiculturalism in my class because we played rap?" This inclusion of poetry needs to connect to the kids' lives and their broader understanding of how language is used to express feelings

in every culture. If there is not a concrete purpose to the lesson, the intention
could be lost.

I would like to explore positive-negative aspects of rap, why it is popular, to get
students to discriminate between positive [and] negative [and] to realize when
something is appropriate or not.

Other teachers cited such issues as navigating cultural stereotypes, rap's
misogyny, and homophobia as possible deterrents to using it in the classroom. They also identified the use of expletives and the term "nigger," as
well as the glorification of violence as potential trouble spots. I noticed
that the teachers spoke about misogyny, homophobia, and violence in a
decontextualized fashion. All three are interwoven into the fabric of the
United States and have been since the inception of the country. They are
also omnipresent in the global community. Therefore, to speak about the
insidiousness of rap, without addressing the society in which it is generated, confirms the claim that the polemics of race and class place rap on
its own terrain and make it a more frequent and visible target (hooks
1994; Rose 1994). Further, within the context presented, Black and Latino
men may express the belief that they are stripped of even basic dignity in
the United States (especially as instances of police brutality, criminalization,
and systematic warehousing in the prison industrial complex steadily increase). Thus, there is a perceived need by some men of color to validate
and affirm a masculine identity by distancing themselves from both women
and gays. While I do not defend this position, I understand it nonetheless.

Yet, it appears as if when rappers discuss the violence in their communities and that perpetuated against them in the forms of police brutality
and capitalism, mainstream America is quick to identify that "they" are
the problem. A prime example of this tendency would be the release of
Ice-T's "Cop Killer," a rap that speaks about police brutality and its potential consequence. Many mainstream critics came out against the song
and artist so forcefully that Time Warner (the conglomerate that produced the record) chose to distance itself from the project. Another outcome of such criticism was the formation of subsidiaries (record labels
financially sustained by conglomerates) that were devoted to the cultiva-
tion of rap projects solely. In this fashion, profits could still be generated,
but huge entertainment corporations would not suffer the backlash of
public outcry.

In another instance (the death of hip hop artist Tupac Shakur), many
within the electronic and print media were quick to note that Tupac died
as he lived, violently. In my mind, there is no doubt that Tupac was both

a target and agent of oppression as we all might be considered. Notice-ably absent from the criticism, however, was the role that corporate America played in constructing the image of Tupac as "thug" and the manner in which it greatly profited from that construction.

Conversely, I found it interesting that, in the case of the varied school shootings and particularly that occurring at Colombine High, mainstream America seemed to see those violent incidents (committed by young, White males) as opportunities to reflect upon society and the ways in which we can better serve the needs of "our" children, as noted by Orlando Patterson in an article in the *New York Times*, 30 April 1999.

Another basic concern was using this controversial music in a delicate manner that would not invoke the ire of administrators, parents, and community members who didn't view it in a positive light. Yet, as with any controversial literature, administrators and parents should be made integral parts of the decision-making process, from the beginning. Also, an alternate lesson should be provided for students whose parents wish to exercise their right to exempt their children from such a lesson.

While I respected the teachers' candor and their willingness to share their views with me, I also believed that the comments (like those asking to teach students to discriminate between good and bad rap) were reflec-tive of dispositions and attitudes that could prove counterproductive in the classroom and contribute to the oppositional divide present in some of their classrooms.

It was difficult for a number of the teachers to grasp the fact that many of their students viewed rappers as respected cultural workers in commu-nities for which "being 'within community' requires more than residence, it requires moral action and political praxis" (James 1993, 36). Such communities also value the ability to "drop science" (speak truth and disseminate wisdom) orally. A number of rappers critique society. Histori-cally, they have attempted to raise the level of consciousness among their "peoples."

For these reasons, rap is a viable site for the practice of *critical media literacy*. Critical media literacy is defined as a means through which to "provid[e] individuals access to understand . . . how print and nonprint texts that are part of [their] everyday live[s] help to construct their knowl-edge of the world and the various social, economic and social positions they occupy within it" (Alvermann et al. 1999, 1–2).

Additionally, the study of critical media literacy enables the reader to study popular culture as both, a site of inquiry and one of pleasure. The study of popular culture usually moves between two spheres, the aesthetic (the artistry and beauty associated with a piece) and the sociohistorical dimensions of the piece (Rose 1994). It is difficult to examine popular culture through both sets of lenses.

In an effort to best serve the teachers with whom I work, assist them in more effectively infusing students cultures in the classroom, and resist the temptation of resorting to didacticism, I engaged them in a two-tiered process. Concomitantly, I desired to provide the teachers with concrete ways in which to move beyond using rap as mere validation to viewing it as a site of inquiry. These objectives were best accomplished by involving the teachers in a culturally synchronous activity focused on rap and critical thought.

Rap and Critical Media Literacy

I determined that I would lead the teachers through an exercise that they would be able to replicate, with modifications, in their respective classrooms. Groups, with four to six participants in each, were formed. Half of the groups were provided with video monitors and a choice of two or three rap videos. The other half were provided with audio cassette players and two rap audio selections. Each group was directed to select a preference that they wished to explore further. In a number of instances, they had to play the tapes a couple of times before determining their choice.

Subsequently, they were provided with a set of questions that would guide their group discussions. These questions were modifications of questions used by Alvermann, Moon, and Hagood in *Popular culture in the classroom: Teaching and researching critical media literacy* (1999).

Participants were actively engaged in responding to the sheet and in debate regarding interpretations and subtexts. In one instance, there was a reference to some preferring to "switch than fight" in Public Enemy's "Fight the Power." The group kept replaying the verse, attempting to determine the identity of a speaker and the exact wording of the quote. Then, one of the White, middle-aged, male members of the group placed the voice as belonging to Martin Luther King, Jr. and the slogan as being popular during the 1960s. As a result of that bit of information, the group was able to infer that the rap was speaking about power in a much broader political context than originally envisioned.

During debriefing, we further explored connections and questioned images and meanings. For example, one group (that was multiracial and varied in respect to life experience) selected Jay-Z's video "Hard knock life." The music samples verses from the score of the Broadway musical "Annie." Participants made connections by using prior knowledge about the musical and attempting to decipher potential reasons for incorporating the selection into the music track and video.

Some members stated that Annie had been able to escape her life circumstances because a rich White man removed her from an unfavorable environment. They contrasted that image with Jay-Z, who had all the accoutrements of wealth (e.g., a Bentley, Rolex watch), but he was unable to help his people out of the ghetto. Other participants mentioned that they were troubled by the materialism and focus on wealth as a sole measure of success, especially when there are limited opportunities for attaining such wealth in communities such as those shown in the video. Yet, I question the focus on consumption within such communities when it might be viewed as symptomatic of a broader societal disease.

Participants from another group stated that the absence of such materialism was a hidden pleasure received as they watched the Fugees' "Killing me softly" (a remake of Roberta Flack's rendition of the same name) with its perceived emphasis on nostalgia, community, and fun.

Another group chose to focus on the imagery and symbolism used by the Fugees in their video collage. They noticed that, in one scene, a Black prisoner and a White police officer were engaged in physical conflict. Both were blinded in one eye. This image led the group to ponder the concepts of justice and oppression. Are they real or perceived? Is justice blind? Why were both men blind in one eye only? Was it an issue of accepting alternative viewpoints and ways of interpreting the world? Possibly, the way in which those interpretations conflict and contest each other?

Through the use of this exercise, participants were able to ascertain that there are different genres of rap; for example, socially conscious rap (that focuses on the big issues like racism, poverty, and consciousness), and ghetto storytellin' or reality rap that chronicles life in U.S. ghettos. There is also rap that focuses primarily on "playin' the dozens as a form of signification." Signification is defined by linguist Geneva Smitherman (1977, 121) as having the following characteristics: indirection, circumlocution; images rooted in the everyday, real world; humor, irony; directed at person or persons usually present in the situational context.

For example, one group listened to an especially provocative rap done by a female hip hop artist. In their discussion, they considered her verbal jousting with a male rap artist and her boasts about her independence and sexual prowess. They engaged in a lively debate regarding whether the claims were feminist in nature or they merely reinforced negative stereotypes of women and confused freedom and self-actualization with dominance.

Conversely, another group listened to Queen Latifah's "U.N.I.T.Y." and explored similar issues of female empowerment. While some group members were put off by the hook (refrain), "You're not a bitch or a ho," others interpreted the piece as a 1990s version of Aretha Franklin's "RESPECT," and one to which their students might more fully relate.

We also discussed the genres of gangsta/hardcore rap and the very harsh light in which they are cast, with some degree of legitimacy. We spoke about the evolution of gangster imagery in the United States. Many of the teachers had not made the connection that, for other immigrant groups like the Irish and Italians, gangster imagery had also proven pleasurable and marketable in respect to popular culture, such as the movies, television, and mass-marketed books.

Finally, we explored the language and the ways in which it empowers and disempowers. The teachers with whom I was meeting were linguistically disempowered by the rap that was used. In this fashion, I could attempt to have them more fully comprehend and empathize with the disadvantage their bidialectical and bilingual students frequently feel in Standard American English-Only classrooms. We dialogued about the nature of expletives and the class implications associated with their use, as well as code switching (in respect to the word "nigger") to explain that it conveys one meaning within a group, yet takes on a totally different one when used outside of the group. We spoke about this practice as used by other racial and ethnic groups also.

Most significantly, we inquired into the cultural implications of using rap's violence, misogyny, and homophobia for didactic purposes (to teach students about the evils of rap from the teacher's vantage point) rather than leading students to reflect upon this art form (site of pleasure) and critique it on their own terms, drawing their own conclusions.

The benefit of these dialogues with teachers has been that they are exposed to a new way through which to potentially approach students and culturally syncretize literacy instruction. Additionally, they have received a chance to critically explore significant issues attached to language, culture, and power through texts to which students relate in their everyday lives.

Note: An earlier version of this chapter was published in the *Journal of Adolescent and Adult Literacy.*

Chapter 8

"Do Unto Others" Schooling

One December evening, I attended a forum on democracy and the plight of public education, hosted by Montclair State University's College of Education and Human Services. Such discussions are accepted and routine within our college. The labors of Dean Michelli and his administration, in this respect, have gained national recognition. As a matter of course, I enjoy these sustained dialogues. I am appreciative of the insights shared and thought provoked.

On this particular evening, the Dean initiated discussion with the proposition: the notion of schools as, undoubtedly, democratic is an essentially contestable contention. It is a premise that is readily accepted; but, it should be challenged. A number of responses were presented. Yet, I remember two most distinctly because they speak to a feeling of ambivalence that arises within me during such exchanges, specifically, and when analyzing the condition of public education, generally.

At one point, a White female administrator stated that viewing the schools as antidemocratic is a depressing assessment and "we won't go there." This instance was not the first during which I heard the acknowledgment of disenfranchisement and inequity characterized as depressing. While attending a Socialist Scholars conference, a speaker pronounced that those of us on the far left are a "really pessimistic group." Whenever I hear this expressed sentiment, I think . . . you know what, the synergy of racism, class bias, sexism, and corresponding injustices *is*, without a doubt, real fuckin' depressing. Living, as these dynamics continually play themselves out in one's existence, *is* real fuckin' depressing.

A Latina colleague also shared during the evening. She stated that our students know that "we're full of . . . you know" as they quickly discern our struggle with the actualization of democracy in the schools. I clearly understood her points and appreciated her candor. But, I took exception to her use of "we." After all, "we" (many of those sitting in that room and to whom she directed her comments) routinely discuss the concept, make efforts to comprehensively understand it, and advance it in the schools for the benefit of *all* students.

Who is truly full of "it" when it comes to the perpetuation of injustice and disempowerment in schools? Potentially, they are those who prompt supposedly color-blind, school policy initiatives that privilege meritocracy, maintain the status quo, and preserve the dis-education of Black and Latino masses. "Dis-education," a term used to characterize the educational encounters of Black and Latino students, is defined as "the experience [of] pervasive, persistent, and disproportionate underachievement in comparison to . . . White counterparts" (Carruthers 1994, 45).

Although both comments were flawed, they spoke to the same point. Those who are critical of schools and public education, regardless of affiliation with the far left or the far right, have little difficulty identifying problems. Quite infrequently, however, does transformative change serve as the focal point. Seldom are the roles discussants play in change agentry explored. "Educational policies and practices were and are the results of struggles and compromises" (Carlson and Apple 1998, 11).

The comments bandied that evening gave rise to another thought as well. For me, they reinforced a chasm existent between many Whites and people of color, which commonly manifests itself in incompatible views on race, democracy, and the ways in which those conceptualizations play themselves out. Additionally, participation in the forum advanced my concern: "Would the endemic and permanent natures of racism and classism ever be truly acknowledged as *primary* factors in the inequitable educational experiences received in the nation's public schools?

These questions led me to meditate upon my own experiences as a public school educator, who chose to work in the urban center solely. I contemplated the point at which I became conscious of the roles schools play in the disenfranchisement of people of color, as well as the impact of the realization on my philosophical orientations toward education and schooling. Ultimately, I was compelled to explore ways in which I might work, more effectively, to prompt change in the urban schools to which I *remain* committed.

Musings on Real Life in Urban Public Schools

My decision to teach was not predicated upon an undying love of children. Instead, I *loved* my subject matter of English/journalism. Generally, I respect children. I, also, hold the firm conviction that they deserve the best that life has to offer. Within that context, each child deserves the best education the United States has to extend.

My most immediate need, following college, was to repay educational debts incurred. The guidance of a male professor, who first suggested that I return home and teach in the public schools, will always be remembered. Against the admonitions of my mother, I commenced teaching through an alternate certification route. Simply stated, the need for teachers reached crisis proportions as the New York City student population steadily grew. This emergency state continues to exist in urban centers throughout the United States.

Although I possessed a college degree, I had not the benefit of a single college-level course focused on education or literacy development. The development of pedagogical strategy was trial and error, as was classroom management. I more fully discuss these processes in a book chapter entitled *Toward developing a multicultural perspective* in Violet Harris' edited collection, *Using multiethnic literature in the K–8 classroom* (1997).

The intermediate school to which I was assigned was relatively new and located in the Southeast Bronx. The principal, a White male attorney with a hulking presence, had been remarkably successful in securing additional equipment and funding, as well as a staff notably exceptional. The school's physical plant was brightly colored, clean, well lit, and well maintained. The faculty was predominantly White, while the student population was predominantly Black and Latino.

Many of the children we taught were from poor and working-class families. But, contrary to popular belief, they were clean, wore beautiful clothes, and had many of the latest technological gadgets. Routinely, they spoke of video games purchased for them, as well as telephones, televisions, and VCRs in their rooms. It was apparent to all that these children were, generally, loved and well cared for. Within that school building, I continually felt that parents, teachers, administrators and support and maintenance staff essentially worked in partnership for the benefit of the children.

While continuing to teach during the day, I pursued graduate studies in education during the evenings. I began to feel much more confident in the classroom. I was given appropriate educational and literacy development terminology to explain the instructional strategies I implemented. Additionally, I was able to cite theory that substantiated my pedagogical decision making. It was around this time that I was first exposed to multicultural education theory and practice as defined by Banks, Gay, Grant, and Sleeter.

Such theory spoke to my life experiences, my experiences as a student, and those as a classroom teacher, in an unparalleled fashion. For instance, I was plagued by the discrepancy between the academic concepts my "remedial" students learned and were capable of learning in the classroom and their unexplained lack of sustained and demonstrable progress on standardized tests. Feeling somewhat insecure as a new teacher, I solely attributed their failure to my inadequate pedagogical knowledge and burgeoning (yet not fully actualized) teaching skills. Multicultural theory assisted me in slowly realizing that my direct role was only one in many that sustained failure for a number of my students. According to theory, factors like poverty, "remedial" students frequently taught by the least experienced teachers, the practices of tracking and ability grouping, as well as the flawed assumptions inherent in and implications of standardized testing, might also have necessitated consideration and analysis.

Yet, as a young woman, I was much less inclined to question the relationships between racism, classism, and the preservation of societal inequity. Instead, I accepted them as evils that would always exist and that I had little personal power to change. Rather than focusing on racism as institutional, I viewed it in terms of hateful, insensitive acts or scourges that should be purged from my students' reading texts.

I exposed the behavior of colleagues who consistently belittled children of color. I challenged colleagues on the use of racist books with their classes. I mentally noted the teachers who made record numbers of special education referrals, especially of Black and Latino boys, and I clandestinely provided parents with the language to successfully postpone and abort special education placements they felt were unwarranted.

Surprisingly, however, a number of my White colleagues did the same. They frequently confronted and ridiculed the teachers we deemed as racist, incompetent, or both. Colleagues, across positionalities, "outed" teachers, regardless of race, who were insensitive and appeared to collude in the colonization of students of color.

To Hell and Back

Then, I went to hell . . . figuratively. Unwittingly, I accepted the position of communication arts teacher trainer. It served as both consolation prize and promotion. Although I had applied to work in the district office (upon the urging of an administrator within the office), I was denied the position and offered another. The denial, a source told me, was based upon a book, entitled *Think and Grow Rich: A Black Choice* (Kimbro and Hill 1991). After reading it en route to the meeting, I naively placed it on the desk next to me as I interviewed. Upon observation of the book title, the interviewer allegedly deemed me "too militant" to work in the district office. As I write, the book remains on the bookshelf closest to my desk as a keepsake and reminder.

My militancy gained me assignment to an embattled school in a high-poverty zone. The school stood in the heart of the South Bronx, not far from Yankee Stadium. Urban decay seemed to engulf me, as I regularly walked to work from the subway station. Customarily, I was so disgusted about the walk to work and that which I encountered in the school building that I was absent. In fact, I became physically ill more times during the course of my year-long employment at the elementary school than I ever had prior or have since.

Ghetto Schools and the Process of Change

The school building in which I worked was old, poorly lit, and in ill repair. Yet, there were respective rooms that teachers and staff had made beautiful with brightly colored decorations and students' work. Although it was the 1990s, school equipment was run down and there were relatively few computers in the school, in contrast to the previous school in which fully equipped computer labs were existent and all administrators had access to computer technology.

Upon arrival to the school, it was easily detected that many of the children's textbooks were copyrighted in the 1970s. Yet, during the course of the year, the principal altered the school's literacy program (upon district recommendation) and, with my assistance, began to acquire numerous class sets of multicultural children's trade books. The books ordered could be considered the best in the field. While it might have been conjectured that teachers would be pleased to receive the new books, many were not. They viewed them as impositions as they would be required to use them rather than aids to enhance students' learning. I was baffled by this position.

Our principal was a Black woman. The faculty, composed predominantly of Blacks and Latinos, seemed to sense the principal's powerlessness to truly effect change or fully support them in their efforts. They treated her as such. Even the assistant principal appeared to give her a vote of no confidence, as evidenced by her comments to teachers. An example of the blatant contempt routinely shown our principal could be evidenced in the following scenario. One day, a faculty conference was called. As the principal spoke, a Black female teacher abruptly and loudly turned her chair so that her back faced the principal. Then she said, audibly, "I ain't listenin' to this bitch," as she proceeded to complete paperwork. The principal feigned composure and continued as if the comment hadn't been heard by many seated in the room.

Mentally, I have often juxtaposed this image with that of my former principal. At one point, it had been related to him (by a group of special education auditors) that a teacher referred to special education students as the "special dead" while other students were present. Our principal responded by using a portion of the monthly faculty conference to discuss the comment and its inappropriateness, especially as he considered that there were a number of "special education teachers" on staff. He elaborated, stating that some teachers were "learning disabled." This group was unable to complete mandated paperwork, follow directions, or meet submission deadlines. Subsequently, he described those who could be classified as "emotionally handicapped." He depicted the group as unable to control their classes, incapable of sensitivity to children's needs, and composed of a number of teachers whose deficient interpersonal skills had resulted in multiple marriage partners. While teachers mumbled and talked about him out of hearing distance, no one directly challenged him on the point during that meeting. In composing this piece, I wonder about the extent to which his white male privilege assisted in his facile acquisition and retention of power.

At my former school, our principal was also commanding in respect to the establishment and maintenance of control over both students and faculty. Many viewed the order as significant and necessary. Its absence placed us all in jeopardy, especially as knives, machetes, and guns routinely made their way into the school building. Numerous accounts of school violence and teacher assault circulated the city; yet at that particular site, many of us felt secure.

Further, if the truth be told, many of us dealt consistently with a few children who could best be characterized as quite "unlovely." I would clarify by stating that the group was not "unlovely" because of any inherent flaws, but rather the lives they lived. For many of us, it was difficult to looking lovingly upon a sixth grade student who stood before his teacher and shattered every window in her car with a baseball bat. It was even more absurd to be expected to treat the student "with fairness" as he was returned to class the next day because the incident in question occurred after three o'clock, the time of official school dismissal. Trust me on this one, it becomes near impossible to speak positively about a child who stands at the school's entrance and systematically announces to all entering the school building that his teacher "don't never wear no panties." Most significantly, it is insufferably painful to love a child who sits in your classroom each day, smiling and coming to you for affirmation, as a city-wide police investigation is conducted in an effort to find him (the anonymous suspect) on charges involving the sexual assault and murder of a little girl, no more than five years of age.

Our principal had a distinct way of using his stellar knowledge of school law and policy to relieve teachers of unlovely children and build effective cases against them. The desired outcome identified as maintaining order and calm.

Conversely, although the children were younger in the new setting, our female principal was often unable to really fight for those things needed to improve the school because her own position could best be described as tenuous. In many ways, she had been rendered ineffective by the disrespect with which her superiors treated her.

On the Job Training

As I had very little staff development in my new role as communication arts teacher trainer, I approached it in the same trial-and-error fashion that I had applied in teaching. Staff development through the district office was, usually, focused on a specific administrative task that had to be accomplished. Little (if any) support was provided. But, I remain grateful to the principal for allowing me to share my ideas with her and her willingness to work toward their implementation. Her efforts to assist me, however, were not well received by a number of those on the faculty. There were complaints and efforts to sabotage. Some teachers threw memorandums I issued in the trash (in my presence). Others chose to attack me personally. While there were staff members who were supportive of my efforts, it appeared as if many teachers linked undesirable, recent changes and demands to my presence. They made their views known. Promotion should come from within the ranks. Also, they saw me as young, arrogant, and elitist. I was an outsider and, in fairness, I had not made efforts to reach out because of my own insecurities and issues. Condemnation was also heaped upon me because of the quasi-administrative nature of my position. Although I had been assigned the task of helping several new teachers, I was also required to report their progress. Eventually, a well-informed decision was made against two of them returning to the school during the subsequent year. While the decision was not mine, it was associated with and supported by me.

While relations with the staff were tense, I truly liked the school's children. They were poor and experienced more than their fair share of health crises, academic challenges, and social problems. But, they were bright and I enjoyed the time I spent with them. I walked away with fresh insights as a result of our discussions. For example, during reading group, my students and I read Mildred Taylor's *The Gold Cadillac*. The story is set during the 1930s or 1940s. It focuses upon a Black family with a new car as they travel through the Jim Crow South. The car impacts their already precarious status as they travel. I talked about the situation as a past injustice and expressed middle-class faith in the criminal justice system. My young students chastised me for this sanguine view of law enforcement, saying "Teacher, that happens today in my hood." They cited many examples of arrests and assaults by police officers, characterized as unjustified and unwarranted.

There were a number of bright spots like this one in which I learned. But, slowly, I began to hate the building, the poverty I recognized, and the realization that a larger number of Black and Latino teachers than I previously believed colluded in the dis-education of our people. Most significantly, I hated the fact that I would do almost anything to avoid going to work. In December (after four months of being there), I decided that I would not return the next year.

Toward a New View of Urban Education

As a result of my experiences in both schools, I began to see, more clearly, the strong connections between communities, cultures to which students ascribed, and the educations they ultimately received. Today, I carry the collective of stories and examples shared as I speak about public education or sit quietly in contemplation of it.

After leaving the public schools and assuming a position in academia, I had more time to truly reflect upon that which I saw in the public schools. Over the course of the next several years, I actively sought new theory that would help, once again, to validate and confirm my thoughts as this approach had worked for me in the past.

In the process, I fell into a trap routinely set for progressive educators. I became disenchanted with multicultural education for all the wrong reasons. Banks (1994) and Grant and Sleeter (1994) had framed complex models of multicultural education in which social action and social reconstruction served as the most sought-after goals of the movement. My disillusionment, however, focused on that which I perceived as the watering-down of multicultural education's strength as some converted it to mere "cultural tourism," a term used by Derman-Sparks (1995). I was also dismayed by the privileging of universality solely. I felt that I'd lose my mind if I heard one more elementary school teacher state, "we are more alike than we are different. After all, we have mommies and daddies, and we all bleed red blood." In many respects, this statement irritated me because I viewed it as a misguided and condescending attempt to convince the dominant group that people of color are human. Such efforts reinforce privilege and the unequal distribution of power.

I also became disenchanted with the attempts of some scholars to make every type of disadvantage of equal importance, when (in my mind) some outweighed others. There was no way in which someone would convince me that disempowerment as a result of weight and height was similar to the gradual and systematic assault on people of color that remains on-going and ubiquitous.

Concomitantly, I was first exposed to critical pedagogy. Critical theorists (like Freire, Bernstein, Bourdieu and Passeron, Macedo, Giroux, McLaren, and hooks) have asserted that schools are sites of cultural and societal inequity. Their claims have suggested that schools replicate societal structures of privilege, domination, and oppression. Critical pedagogy also seemed to accommodate my political beliefs, as I identify myself as a Democratic Socialist. The classification is a means of acknowledging that the American ideal of democracy has not yet been fully actualized. My self-identification helps to distinguish that I have difficulty listening to the virtues of the country's founding fathers when I know that, in spite of privileging liberty and defining democracy, they never envisioned me nor those who look like me as beneficiaries of their toils.

I identify myself as a Democratic Socialist, in an effort to strike against the rampant consumerism and avarice that have served as the natural outcomes of capitalism. While current statistics identify that the country is in great fiscal health with both employment and spending up, huge sectors in communities of color remain disadvantaged and poor (even though they might work each day). "The unequal distribution of wealth under capitalism—in which the top 1 percent of all households has a greater net wealth than the bottom 90 percent—makes liberty a function of power, privilege, and control" (Marable 1996, 272).

There are a number of readers who might find my public acknowledgment of Socialist proclivities questionable or misguided with the collapse of the Cold War, the death of the Soviet Union, and "capitalist triumphalism" spreading throughout the world (Marable 1996, 269). I am also cognizant that historically, Marxists, Communists, and Socialists have placed class before race in their struggles and abandoned our interests if their own were in danger of subjugation. Traditionally, Blacks and Latinos have also had difficulty with Marxism's atheistic dimensions (Marable 1996).

Yet, in my identification, I use Marable's definition of Socialism's new vision. He defines it "as a radical project for democratic change" (270) and focused on "the commitment to human equality" (272).

However, while I have realized the virtues of critical pedagogy and theory and found it closely aligned with my own political beliefs, I have come to the understanding that it, like its theoretical counterparts, serves as no panacea. The same criticisms that have been made about Communism, Marxism, and socialism traditionally also seem to apply to progressive educators and critical pedagogy. In reading work recently that discussed the directions of radical pedagogy and rifts that had developed between critical and feminist pedagogues (Gore 1998, 271–288; Carlson and Apple 1998, 1–38), I counted the citations that I could identify as belonging to people of color and remained plagued by a long-standing question: "Why is it that, even in progressive camps, the voices of Whites, generally, and White males specifically, remain privileged?" To use the imagery of Spike Lee in his film *Do The Right Thing* and the words of his character Buggin' Out: "Put some [more] brothers [and sisters] on the wall!" This cry represents self-representation, "and can easily be translated into a larger demand for self-determination," (Boyd 1995, 155). In many ways that leads me to wonder about the ability of the rhetoric to live up to the reality. It is for this reason that I have chosen to align myself with a number of other educators who actively work toward taking the best of multicultural education, critical pedagogy, and feminist theory and applying them to U.S. education and schooling, in the form of "liberatory pedagogy" (Gordon 1995; Lawrence 1995).

I don't wish to define "liberatory pedagogy" with clear, definite boundaries, causing some to identify it (perhaps aptly) as essentialist, as the process of naming anything is imprecise. It is necessary, however, as a means of self-determination.

There are those who will contend that Paulo Freire was the first to connect the terms "liberation" with "pedagogy" (Shor 1987). While I do not deny that Freire popularized this link, I also recognize Woodson's contribution to it and his words in *The mis-education of the Negro* (1933). I remember quotes such as: "It is merely a matter of exercising common sense in approaching people through their environment in order to deal with conditions as they are rather than as you would like to see them or imagine that they are" (xi) and "But can you expect teachers to revolutionize the social order for the good of the community? Indeed we must expect this very thing" (145).

I use the term "liberatory pedagogy" consciously and as a means through which to question the fact that critical and feminist pedagogues have oftentimes seemed to place the interests of people of color on the periphery or as an afterthought. In a number of instances, they also have chosen to assume the empowering position of speaking for us rather than truly sharing power with us. In order to establish parity, we must be more fully supported in speaking for ourselves and representing ourselves. Interest convergence can only actualize as all parties represented are viewed as true equals.

Further, I use the term "liberatory pedagogy" as a way of acknowledging the brilliance of Carter G. Woodson, Anna Julia Cooper, and W.E.B. DuBois and their contributions to the definition of progressive education within U.S. borders. It is a means by which to acknowledge the Sabbath Schools of Reconstruction-era, the Freedom Schools, Citizen Schools, and Highlander Folk School of the modern-day Civil Rights period, as well as the efforts of teachers like Septima Clark, Myles Horton, Esau Jenkins, and Fannie Lou Hamer. I wish to challenge the way in which White educators, even those who are progressive and liberal, have been much more open to innovative educational philosophies dealing with issues of race and class outside of the U.S. than deal with collective racism and its historic legacy, the sustained negation of Black intellectuals and Black epistemology within its borders.

Liberatory pedagogy emphasizes political praxis and approaches Black subject matter and that involving people of color in an empathic and culturally sensitive fashion. It displays commitment to human equality, social justice, and coalition-building. Liberatory pedagogy, theory, and practice, focuses on issues of parity like those of curriculum, instruction, assessment, school funding, and desegregation (Ladson-Billings 1999). Its purpose is to extirpate all forms of oppression from the public domain of schools (Tate 1999).

Finally, liberatory pedagogy is focused on hope and possibility. It is centered on "the language of possibility . . . the terrain of hope and agency, to the sphere of struggle and action, one steeped in a vision which chooses life and offers constructive alternatives" (Aronowitz and Giroux 1985, 19).

Responses

As mentioned in the prologue, this book has a transformative agenda. In that spirit, I wished to present individual readers with the opportunity to respond to this text from their various positionalities and perspectives. Specifically, I sought responses from a Black woman, a White woman, a Black man, and a White man. I have secured all with the exception of one, the response from a Black man. The fact that the response did not make it to publication is the result of a myriad of situational variables and decisions. Yet, I wish to state quite emphatically that the response was desired and there was never an attempt to exclude this significant voice.

Response One

On March 25, 1999, I was addressing faculty of our university on a day set aside to reflect on democracy and democratic practice. A colleague from Anthropology had presented a summary of his work in Kerela, the Indian state often cited as a model for democratic practice, characterized by high literacy, low infant mortality, and broad community action to enhance the quality of life. I began my remarks by saying that Dierdre Glenn Paul, one of the faculty members in our college, was absent. She was, I reported, probably under arrest. She had chosen to engage in an act of civil disobedience to protest the killing of Amadou Diallo by a group of New York City Police Department officers. While we are talking about social justice and democracy, I said, Dr. Glenn Paul is doing it.

This book is enlightening, yet unsettling and disturbing. Glenn Paul chronicles her own experiences as "a Black woman living in a racially schizophrenic society," with pain so pervasive that it is hard to "distinguish between the pain resulting from status as Black or female." Whether she is reporting on her perception of television as an "electronic auction block," her experiences in meetings, or her early interactions with her students, she is able to remind us repeatedly of how far we have to go to achieve the ideal of social and political democracy. Even in a setting where the theme is the promotion of democratic practice and social justice, we find individuals who, through words and actions, violate the principles we seek to expand. Perhaps it is especially important to have someone like Dr. Glenn Paul present when the overt goal is the promotion of democracy, because the language of democracy is seductive. It is much easier to talk about than to act on, and her ability to focus on action is a critically important catalyst to bring about change in the way we all live our lives rather than the way we talk about how we would like to live our lives. Glenn Paul is able, in these pages and in the way she leads her life, to keep us focused and remind us when we slip.

I am reminded of one of my favorite passages from Tocqueville, the young French aristocrat who in his nine months in the United States in 1831 managed to capture some of the promise and enduring problems of democracy. Tocqueville comments on how compelling the concept of being free is, and then reminds us that "there is nothing more arduous than the apprenticeship of liberty." "Liberty," he writes, "is generally established with difficulty in the midst of storms; it is perfected by civil discord; and its benefits cannot be appreciated until it is already old." Put this together with Benjamin Barber's assertion that "democracy is not a natural form of association, it is an extraordinary and rare contrivance of cultivated imagination" (5) and we realize how fragile our democracy is. Dierdre Glenn Paul reminds us that we must reinvent democracy with each new generation, especially in the ways we would treat and respect each other and in our conception of social justice. Further, we must constantly test ourselves about our convictions. She compels us to use all of our powers of persuasion, especially as educators, to examine not just the issues, but our lives, in pursuit of the kind of life we would wish for all. This attention of education to the rekindling, the maintenance, and the enhancement of democracy is largely absent in American schools, and so it is not surprising that she encounters students who do not reflect the democratic dispositions and values we embrace. By and large, they have not experienced them. Her commitment as a teacher educator to prepare teachers who will not forget this obligation is compelling.

Glenn Paul's qualities as an educator are readily apparent in this book. A central theme of our program to prepare teachers is "critical thinking." One of Glenn Paul's significant contributions has been her persistence in expanding critical thinking to include social action—a natural extension of her and our commitment to critical, liberatory pedagogy. In this way, she takes talk about critical thinking to a new plane, from being an intellectual exercise to transforming ourselves and society. Her analysis of her own pedagogy and her ability to be reflective and modify behavior is a lesson for us all. She introduces us to rap as a cultural artifact and pedagogical tool. She shares with us her growing appreciation of diversity as she becomes more involved with her students' stories. She recognizes that, in her early teaching efforts, "despite my self description as a radical teacher, some of the methods I used silenced my students." She does not, however, give up or sell out. Understanding that democracy and democratic practice must be rekindled in each new generation, and that, hard as this effort is, it is essential, especially with our young citizens who would be teachers.

Another important aspect of this book is her conception of what it means to be an intellectual. To Glenn Paul, an intellectual is one who is "committed to a life of the mind, the development of a critical consciousness, and political activism." We see examples of how this commitment has played out in her life, from her extraordinary courage in deciding to be steadfast in charging the man who raped her in spite of the consequences to her, to her arrest in New York seeking justice for Amadou Diallo. She reminds us that liberatory pedagogy, pedagogy that leads to social change, has its roots in the work of Anna Julia Cooper, W.E.B. DuBois, and Carter G. Woodson. She uses this to reinforce our tendency, the tendency of White educators in the United States, to embrace ideas like liberatory pedagogy when they are proposed outside the United States, rather than to deal with "collective racism, its historic legacy and sustained negation of Black intellectuals and Black epistemology that have come to pass within the borders of the United States." Glenn Paul, explicitly and by implication, reminds us that we have to think more carefully and critically about words we use and the ways in which we use them as they are open to misinterpretation. We need to be able to talk about different interpretations of both words and actions and understand that people of color see the world through a different racial lens than that used by privileged Whites, but with both sets of lenses shaped by experience. Universities must provide forums for such discussion as we learn new ways to talk to each other.

Not unrelated to the need to understand these different perspectives, there is much focus in American higher education on reconceptualizing the meaning of scholarship, a movement begun by Ernest Boyer and extended by the American Association for Higher Education. Part of this reconceptualization is a focus on the "scholarship of application," which includes using scholarship to solve consequential social problems. Glenn Paul takes us a step beyond that and, with roots in DuBois and Nel Noddings, she describes Black Womanist scholarship that has promise to add a new perspective to the complexities of our society and, indeed, the world.

When she turns to the concepts of Black maternal epistemology, the use of Black images as a manifestation and reinforcement of racism, and her analysis of urban education, she breaks new ground and leaves us wanting to hear more. As she contemplates her own preparedness for motherhood and the choices she makes for her own children, one cannot resist thinking of poor women, Black and White, who have no choices to make. We should examine policies adopted in some states that have the potential to replace Black female caregivers in urban preschool centers who live in the community with others who do not. This may be the unintended outcome of setting policies that on their face raise standards, while establishing conditions that urban residents may have difficulty meeting and therefore replacing them with outsiders? Can the concept of Black maternal epistemology inform intelligent policy decisions that affect young children in such settings? The critical thing for educators is the need to better understand the implications of Black maternal epistemology for the development of children and their learning needs. Dr. Glenn Paul is right when she asserts that "we have so many lessons yet to learn about motherhood written from the perspective of Black mothers." We would do well to enter the door she has opened.

The issue of learning to teach from the perspective of cultural responsiveness, the terrible burdens of racism, and the hope that pedagogy can be liberating form a backdrop for her final chapter. I believe she puts her finger on the most important question we must face in dealing not only with urban education, but with the performance of Black and Hispanic students in most schools, when she says, "I wondered whether the endemic and permanent natures of racism and classism, specifically, would ever be truly acknowledged as primary factors in the inequitable educational experiences received in the nation's public schools." I hope she is wrong when she thinks of racism and classism as permanent, but clearly she is right when she asserts that the effects of both must be taken into account in seeking educational improvement. No system of "whole school reform" can succeed without considering and addressing the pervasive racism and classism that is still evident in our schools. That is one of the reasons that we must prepare future teachers who deeply understand the ideals of American political and social democracy, including especially social justice, and who are prepared to overcome both the achievement gap and the democracy gap.

Reading this book will undoubtedly make many uncomfortable for it raises the issues we often prefer to ignore. Confronting the issues, however, is more than a consequence of making universities more diverse: it is a moral obligation. We must be open to the tensions inherent in diversity. Academia, and the rest of society, must expand its vision of opening up the dialogue to include the perspectives of those who challenge the very foundations of what we believe and how we see ourselves. The author hopes that the book will be transformative, that it will bring about change for those who pursue it, and that we will learn to appreciate the complexity of the work by viewing it through a different set of lenses. She hopes we will become more cognizant of our actions and the dispositions that lead to them. She hopes we will commit to a more rigorous fight for social justice across lines of positionality. Knowing and working with her has had these effects on many, and it is likely that reading and reflecting on this important book will as well.

Nicholas M. Michelli
Dean, College of Education and Human Services
Montclair State University

Response Two

A Journey Too Long, One Crossing Too Many

Upon experiencing *Life, Culture, Education on the Academic Plantation: Womanist Thought and Perspective,* I was transported back to the time my co-editor Kris and I worked on our book, *Everyday knowledge and uncommon truths: Women of the academy* (Christian-Smith & Kellor, 1999). My emotional and physical responses to Dierdre Glenn Paul's book are very similar to what I experienced during those stimulating and draining four years. Once again, I had that tight chest and huge knot in my stomach as the story of yet another woman's struggles in daily life and academe with dignity and respect unfolded before me. Every time I read a chapter from another contributor, the knots and tightness burst forth in anger and outrage. After the final reading of our book, I realized that each chapter represented a "victory narrative" where the smart, capable woman had outwitted her oppressors and went on with her personal and professional life. In my concluding chapter to the book I called them "dark victories" because the experiences, although traumatic and wounding, had become the foundation for theory-building and political action on campus and in the larger world. *Life, Education, Culture* represents such a victory. I will use the word *experience* instead of *read* to describe my entrance into the multiple worlds Dierdre Glenn Paul inhabits. A good book should be a powerful emotional, physical, intellectual and spiritual experience where the words fly out at you like bats, to paraphrase Marx. It should also break silences. *Life, Education, Culture* is such a book.

The chapters in *Life, Education, Culture* did indeed swoop down on me, causing me to experience as much as I could as a White Midwestern woman, Dierdre's early life, education, and years in academe. Dierdre's clear precise writing wove familiar tales about being a studious girl in a working class community. Yet I did not grow up in a Black neighborhood in the Bronx. Nor did I experience the same race, gender, and class struggles for access to power and opportunities. Although I was the object of misunderstanding and ridicule as a young female intellectual from the working class, I was still generally treated with some respect and dignity because of my race. My white skin opened doors that Dierdre and her female relatives had to break down. However, there were common barriers because of our shared social class backgrounds. Dierdre's account of her mother demanding scholarship information reminded me of my mother's confrontation with my high school principal regarding my being passed over for membership into the National Honor Society. This would give me an edge in applying for those all important college scholarships. Our mothers prevailed. Dierdre went to private school and I was inducted into the Honor Society and subsequently received a full scholarship to the University of Minnesota.

Our family lives were sources of strength, but also pain. I, too, have survived abuse inside and outside of the home at the hands of women and men whose dreams had been deferred, to borrow poet Langston Hughes's powerful phrasing. I was the object of intense physical and intellectual control by my parents. My whereabouts were continually monitored and I got hell if I was not where I was supposed to be. I was not a wild girl, but merely adventurous. My parents sought to control my thinking especially as I outfaced my family and neighbors in "book learning." When I voiced my views or questioned those of my parents and other adults, I was a "snotty girl" with "no respect for elders." My age precluded me from knowing what I talked about for I had not walked on earth as long as they had. This holding back of children is not uncommon in the working class as Paul Willis's (1977) and Christine Griffin's (1985) classic studies have shown. Only recently have I learned the motive behind my parents' actions. My mother's dream of becoming a business teacher were thwarted by her parents as she was sent to secretarial school instead of normal school. She was outwardly proud of her daughter and continually stressed the importance of an education, although as something to fall back on if needed. Inside she felt that she was losing control of her daughter and had mixed feelings over her daughter achieving what she could not. Both of my parents were fearful of losing their daughter's devotion because she had ventured far into the world. They realized what I would later learn: How difficult it is to inhabit the worlds of home, work, and scholarship and the necessity of tremendous tradeoffs. However, I resented and still do the means through which this understanding was conveyed.

I now want to expand upon several of the issues raised above. *Life, Culture, Education* is above all an example of Kellor's (1999) notion of embodied theory and practice. Although many have spoken of the importance of "writing the body" (Irigaray 1985), rarely has it been done in such an eloquent manner. Dierdre Glenn Paul's achievements are varied in this regard. Her analyses of the body as physical presence, companion to the emotional and spiritual, contested terrain, object of symbolic, mental, and physical violence and as a social and political discourse to be deconstructed provide a useful framework for other researchers. Here, the body emerges as material and discursive, the site where violence toward women coalesces. Dierdre's accomplishment also is evident in her description and analysis of the body and soul "murder" (Kellor 1999) wrought by the various forms of violence against herself and other Black women. Her sophisticated discussion of unlawful body violation during her college years, the challenge and joys of being a classroom teacher, her marriage, the birth of her children, being arrested at a political protest, and the many incidents of bias and attempted silencing in her workplace may strongly resonate with many readers as it did with myself. These discussions, when linked with the existing scholarship by Black women scholars, form a foundation for Dierdre's important contribution to the theories and practices of Black Womanist Thought.

Violence in its various forms underlies Dierdre's discussion of power and control in society, especially in academe, although not in the usual manner of most White feminist academics. With few exceptions (Cooper and Ideta 1999, Dixon 1998), their discussions have concentrated on the consequences for women of the control of academe by some White men (Aisenberg and Harrington 1986, Roman and Eyre 1997). Feminists have shown great reluctance to broach the subject of women oppressing women, fearful of charges of being "unsisterly" and giving others further cause to discredit women. *Life, Education, Culture* boldly breaks this silence through the discussion of women faculty and administrators who contribute to and condone a hostile work climate and dominate and oppress not only women, but men. This becomes all the more serious when such women profess to be feminists and avow belief in democracy in the workplace while they secretly form coalitions with men and women to oppress other faculty. Dierdre's experiences are mirrored in countless women around the world, including myself, who have worked with these kinds of women faculty and administrators.

Many have worked for the presence of more women in positions of power as a central strategy against the highly bureaucratic and patriarchal organization of many workplaces, academe included. However, what this strategy ignores is the role of dominant patterns of power. To secure administrative or senior positions, many women deliberately or reluctantly assume the dominant culture and modes of control. The power structure of academe is complex and slippery. It is also very resistant to change. For all of its touting of academic freedom and democracy, academe remains a bookworm business where deals are made behind the backs of faculty and the real power brokers may not be those sitting in the big office (Christian-Smith and Kellor 1999). There are many reprisals for breaking the silence regarding these invisible networks. Those who speak publicly and write about these matters like myself and Dierdre are charged with being "immature" and "idealists" and frequently harassed. Other reprisals can include lowering of one's merit ratings for salary increases and even loss of a job. It is no wonder that few women speak candidly of their work experiences. The "grow up" or "get out" messages that Dierdre has received from other academics is yet another method of keeping the silence by discrediting the critic. I consider idealism to be necessary in any workplace, academe notwithstanding. It is the engine for honesty, humaneness, improvement, and compelling the institution to live up to the promises that are contained in university mottoes and mission statements. Without idealism, academe would be a far less humane place for academic workers and students.

Dierdre breaks other silences in this book. Dierdre takes on the politically charged topic of Black men and their roles as oppressors of Black women. This bold move may cause eyebrows to be raised in some circles. Speaking now as a White feminist teacher and political activist, I regard the necessity of men across social classes, races, ethnic backgrounds, and sexual orientations confronting and reflecting on their roles as oppressors of others to be of utmost importance. As a teacher, I work with many women who combine teaching careers with home, children, and other family obligations. They often reveal how their lives are different and similar to that of their mothers: they go out to work and work in their homes. They are overworked on all fronts, especially if a single parent. The men in their lives may not interfere with their careers, but do little to make their lives easier. They may also be supportive of raising strong daughters with career plans, but endorse traditional ideas about how their sons should be and act. I continue to witness young boys enacting traditional patterns of power and control on the playground and in the classroom that put them at odds with attempts to teach them to act in a peaceful manner (Connell 1996). Those like Dierdre who are attempting to raise sensitive, caring, and nonviolent boys are finding it very challenging. The violence perpetrated against women continues to rise and some attribute this to women's changing roles and some men's inability to accept this on a deep level (Faludi 1991). I believe that violence also stems from a central contradiction: society in general has been slow to accept fundamental changes in men's lives and many men still cling to the past and oppose sharing power with women or resent powerful women. I have always viewed the various feminisms as a series of movements for the liberation of people, not merely women. Until those who have power and use violence in its various forms to oppress others have confronted and taken responsibility for their past and present actions while committing themselves to a new course, sweeping social change that will benefit both genders and transform the relations between the social classes, races, and those of varying sexual orientations will not be realized. All lives, including those of men, are diminished by current circumstances.

Critical literacy grounded in critical pedagogy is central to Dierdre's vision of a more egalitarian society composed of active participants in democracy. She is in the tradition of Muspratt, Luke and Freebody (1997) and others who have reconceptualized literacy as a political practice that plays a central role in maintaining social boundaries. Literacy can also have emancipatory dimensions when teachers emphasize its political dimensions and use it as a tool for action in the world. Dierdre provides excellent examples from her own practice of ways that teachers can engage students in political actions that are the essence of critical literacy. While series books such as romances, mysteries, and horror continue to be popular (Christian-Smith 2000), other texts are on the rise as sources of knowledge of self and the world for youth. Dierdre correctly identifies various media including advertising, videos, computer games, and television as the texts of choice for many boys and girls today. Teaching youth how to deconstruct these texts and understand the personal and social impact they may have is not only a key dimension of literacy instruction, but an important strategy for social movements as well. The "fight back" campaigns of Black communities against the manufacturers of alcohol and tobacco whose advertising target Black men and youth is but one strategy to effect social change.

In *Multiplicities* Dierdre Glenn Paul has crossed many borders into areas that Black and other women have occupied as interlopers, at least in the views of those in power and control. The journey described in this book has been a long one for Dierdre and the women before her. I would like to conclude that this journey is almost at its end, but that would not be accurate. Women will continue to cross many borders for many years to come and for them, *Multiplicities* can serve as a series of guideposts marking their way as they make yet another crossing too many.

Linda K. Christian-Smith
The University of Wisconsin, Oshkosh

References

Aisenberg, N. and Harrington, M. (1986). *Woman of academe: Outsiders in the sacred grove*. Amherst, MA: University of Massachusetts Press.

Christian-Smith, L. K. (2000–in press). The politics of literacies: Young women readers. In A. Muspratt, B. Davies, and P. Freebody (eds.), *Literacy education: Difference, silence and cultural practice*. Sydney: Allen Unwin.

Christian-Smith, L. K. and Kellor, K. S. (1999). *Everyday knowledge and uncommon truths: Women of the academy*. Boulder, CO: Westview Press.

Connell, R. W. (1996). Teaching the boys: New research on masculinity, and gender strategies for schools. *Teachers College Record*, 98(2), 206–235.

Cooper, J.E. and Ideta, L.M. (1999). Asian women leaders of higher education: Stories of strength and self-discovery. In L.K. Christian-Smith and K.S. Kellor (1999). *Everyday knowledge and uncommon truths: Women of the academy* (129–146). Boulder, CO: Westview Press.

Dixon, K. (1998). *Outbursts in academe: Multiculturalism and other sources of conflict.* Portsmouth, NH: Boynton/Cook Publishers.

Faludi, S. (1991). *Backlash.* New York: Crown.

Griffin, C. (1985). *Typical girls?* London: Routledge & Kegan Paul.

Irigaray, L. (1985). *Speculum of the other woman.* Ithaca NY: Cornell University Press.

Kellor, K.S. (1999). Her-story: Life history as a strategy of resistance to being constituted woman in academe. In L.K. Christian-Smith and K.S. Kellor (1999). *Everyday knowledge and uncommon truths: Women of the academy* (25–44). Boulder, CO: Westview Press.

Muspratt, S., Luke, A. and Freebody, P. (1997). *Constructing critical literacies.* Cresskill, NJ: Hampton Press.

Roman, L. and Eyre, L. (1997). *Dangerous territories.* New York: Routledge.

Willis, P. (1977). *Learning to labour.* Westmead, Eng: Saxon House.

Response Three

Being a faculty member, living and working in the academy, is as danger-ous as it is rewarding. Being a faculty member living and working in the academy, and an African American and a woman and a mother situates one in both challenges and opportunities, with a perspective unique [un-fortunately] to the institution. You are simultaneously an outsider and an [almost] insider, measured yet immeasurable, normative but still unique and rare. All of these descriptors speak to Dierdre Glenn Paul's *Life, Education, Culture on the Academic Plantation: Womanist Thought and Perspective.*

When Dierdre explained her project to me, particularly asking others to write various responses to the book, I was intrigued. Usually one writes one's own responses, because who better knows you, but you. But this was different—Dierdre, an emerging Black Womanist intellectual, was giv-ing a stranger permission to be an independent reviewer and critic oper-ating inside her own creative artifact of scholarly cultural writing. I use the terms "scholarly" and "cultural" because this book is both a scholarly work, in that she does use academic/scholarly evidence and academic citations to situate her work into a larger body of intellectual arguments, and a cultural work, in that it speaks to her community.

As I proceeded through the book, I spoke to Dierdre about my concerns, the main one being that there are two books here. One that is a scholarly critique of people of color in American education from classrooms to higher education and as part of the academy itself. On the other hand, this work is an ongoing spiritual journey through life, as I described it to Dierdre, a type of Maya Angelou. Dierdre finds herself in a place, not uncommon to Black women, in which she is trying to simultaneously heal, reflect, and share. Surely, a great measure of this is as cathartic exercise.

As we learn, the life of Dierdre Glenn Paul is a weave—kente cloth with various, conflicting, clashing, but also harmonious strands. Her voice grows with the growing number of Black women who use biography and autobiography as a mechanism to teach us and themselves to explore and critically reflect on lives lived, and the triumphs and tragedies of everyday life.

Many sections of the book read like a stream of consciousness, like Jean Toomer's work, rather than highly structured and organized chapters, in which we see Dierdre flow from one topic to another and back again. Sometimes this helps the reader, other times it is confusing and feels contradictory. And yet, she hits the nail directly on the head so many times that it compensates for her weaving back and forth.

Perhaps the most disturbing section of the book deals with the violence in Dierdre's personal life. Obviously, Dierdre is very sensitive to the fact that, in her life history narrative, she has displayed for the academic community to see what went on behind closed doors in her home as a child, a college-aged student, adult, working professional, and mother. Growing up was not easy, but it never is, especially when you begin by "being a problem" as DuBois commented. Growing up when your folks are divorced, and there is difficulty in the home is not easy, but here again, being able to attend an exclusive boarding school in Pittsfield, Massachusetts is not normative within the Black community either. Dierdre's mother, grandmother, and even godmother stand as very strong and powerful influences in the lives of her and her sister. Albeit that her mother is a strong, middle-class woman who holds a privileged education, has ambitious plans for her daughters, and apparently had a positive male role model in her life (her father). Yet, she selected abusive and violent men. Unfortunately, for all of us, the actions of Dierdre's father and stepfather leave not only deep psychological scars on Dierdre, but also lessons that she had to relearn.

In her freshman year at college, she tells of her rape by her "fiancé" and his fraternity brother. Even more than brutal, this act against Dierdre [or any woman] is cruel, and I was delighted to see that, in a university disciplinary hearing, she was able to confront her "fiancé" attacker. For this reader, however, there are many unanswered questions about this incident. Dierdre does not provide the details as to the circumstances surrounding her getting into the spatial situation wherein the rape occurred. It is unclear to me that many Black girls grow up in parallel realities of brutal Black men and rape. Dierdre says the rape was committed by Black men. I say, the tragedy was committed by foolish and bullying college children who gave in to the excesses of hormones, arrogance, and mean-spiritedness, who saw sex as conquest and commodity, and paid the price by ruining at least three lives and perhaps even more. And yes, to an extent, Dierdre was a "participant" in her own abuse, but she regained her footing and personhood. When she states that Black men see Black women as the enemy, as conspiring with Whites in their destruction, the only data she offers to explain these behaviors are her personal experience at the hands of Black men.

In the academy, there is always sniping, always comments, always in Dierdre's words, "the on-going and pervasive racism with which scholars of color must contend on a daily basis and which excludes them from complete and consequential participation in the academy," the academic colonialism (34). Nevertheless, this is the venue in which we have chosen to work, and few of us have had "crystal stairs." Choosing one's battles is prudent, because as Black faculty we do get weary and yes, some of the allegedly academic debates are an effort to negate our presence in the academy! And even if her situation "was often exacerbated by [her] youth, assertiveness, and personal style," Dierdre's responses come from being under siege. Most Black faculty understand too well, the hurt and anger she feels, for as we all know, just because you're paranoid, it doesn't mean that they are not out to get you.

Dierdre's experiences as a volunteer for women's literacy training in jail or as novice teacher in the South Bronx provides wonderful snips of classroom ideas, such as using rap as an entry into poetry, but unfortunately, the book needs to provide more detailed examples of the daily life and pedagogy employed in her classroom. Her insights and critique of the tensions with White teaching faculty are on target, as is her pinpointing the contradiction of the teachers describing rap as misogynistic, violent, and homophobic, while ignoring how these traits are interwoven into the fabric of American life from its inception.

Talking about her successful experiences as an elementary school Communications Arts teacher trainer and feeling more proficient at teaching public school students gives us a glimpse of her "for instances." Talking about the hell she experiences from White, predominantly female, pre- and in-service teachers is nothing new for Black faculty and particularly Black female faculty members. Her descriptions of these universal reverse racism complaints against us, such as, "I don't know what she wants" or "why is there so much multicultural material in this course" are validating for me. Yes, the pre- and in-service teachers are very clever at using course evaluations to spew their venom against having to confront their own racism. Clearly, they reject the pedagogical tools prescribed by Black faculty to help them improve their teaching in urban schools, where they don't want to be, but can't get into suburban or other upscale private K–12 institutions. Moreover, the examples of the few Black and Latino teachers that had seeming course/grade issues with Dierdre are reminders that even when race is not an issue, ideology and commitment to improving one's pedagogical skill, style, and perspective is essential. Perhaps more reflection on Dierdre's part, about how to engage higher education students without being bombastic, without ignoring race, or having to become an honorary White person, while continuing to insist on high standards for all pre- and in-service teachers will help some, but not all of the confrontational situations.

Her discussion of the electronic auction block is on target. Dierdre asks the questions and interrogates the positionality of African Americans in contemporary social media in a way that is sorely needed. The issues of sexual exploitation of Black women and the use of social science to perpetuate Euro-American debauchery puts White male sexual depravity as a main contributing factor in exploitation. Overall, Dierdre gives a great critique of the role of print and electronic media in creating imagery of African Americans in "the new racism," which is perhaps not so new, but just increasingly blatant and lacking remorse. My worry is how many within the community will hear and learn from her insights.

Finally in her chapter on undoing others' schooling, I found refreshingly honest her concept of "dis-education" of Black and Latino students from poor and working class families which are pervasive, persistent, and disproportionate underachievement in comparison to White counterparts and "unlovely children." But, what, if anything, do we do about these "unlovelys"? What happens to them and us? We, too, along with Dierdre struggle with this, not that she can single-handedly solve the problem, but what to do still remains a question. I also loved the way that she challenges assumptions about what poor and working class families do and do not provide for their children. I like her ideas about class practices and pedagogy and her subversive tactics, but again, if possible, I wanted more specifics.

A cathartic exercise may well be the kind of "border" crossing that generates discussion and growth within the African American community, but I fear that the community, writ large, will not be privy to this piece, because it is written for the academic community. Obviously, my fears and misgivings are not limited to *Life, Education, Culture*. It is a fear that I struggle with on an ongoing basis, because it is the life history that frames and contextualizes our work (as Black female scholars) within the academic, cultural, social, personal, and spiritual arenas. When she talks about herself and facial scarring, in contrast to her mother's green eyes, I want to remind her to recall Nancy Wilson's rendition of "Black is Beautiful" because this sister is young, gifted, and Black (to recall Nina Simone's rendition of the song with the same title).

Much of what Dierdre Glenn Paul writes reflects her own working out of issues. Indeed, this book is a "work" in progress, the author herself being the "work" who is reflecting on herself and the world she is confronted with in everyday life. I believe that Dierdre must and will get through this door, and be able to go on. We should all expect great things from her in the future.

Beverly M. Gordon
Ohio State University

Bibliography

Alcoff, L. (1988). Cultural feminism versus post-structuralism: The identity crisis in feminist theory. *Signs* 13(4): 405–436.

Ali, S. (1989). *The Blackman's guide to understanding the Blackwoman.* Philadelphia, PA: Civilized Publications.

Alpert, B. (1991). Student's resistance in the classroom. *Anthropology and Education Quarterly*, 22: 350–366.

Alvermann, D., Moon, J. S., and Hagood, M. C. (1999). *Popular culture in the classroom: Teaching and researching critical media literacy.* Newark, DE: International Reading Association.

Anderson, J. (1978). Northern philanthropy and the training of the Black leadership. In V. P. Franklin and J. Anderson, eds., *New perspectives on Black educational history* (97–111). Boston, MA: G. K. Hall.

Apple, M. W. and Oliver, A. (1998). Becoming right: Education and the formation of conservative movements. In D. Carlson and M. W. Apple, eds. *Power/knowledge/pedagogy: The meaning of democratic education in unsettling times* (123–148). Boulder, CO: Westview Press.

Arce, C. (1978). Chicano participation in academe: A case of academic colonialism. *Grito del Sol: Chicano Quarterly* 3: 75–104.

Aronowitz, S. (1989). Working-class identity and celluloid fantasies in an electronic age. In H. A. Giroux, R. I. Simon, and contributors. *Popular culture, schooling and everyday life* (197–217). Westport, CT: Bergin & Garvey.

Aronowitz, S. and Giroux, H. A. (1985). *Education under siege.* South Hadley, MA: Bergin & Garvey.

Au, K. H., Carroll, J. H., and Scheu, J. A. (1997). *Balanced literacy instruction: A teacher's resource book.* Norwood, MA: Christopher-Gordon Publishers, Inc.

Bambara, T. C. (1996). *Deep sightings and rescue missions: Fiction, essays, and conversations.* New York: Pantheon Books.

Banks, J. A. (1992). African American scholarship and the evolution of multicultural education. *Journal of Negro Education* 61(3): 273–286.

————— (1995). Multicultural education: Historical development, dimensions, and practice. In J. A. Banks and C.A.M. Banks, eds., *Handbook of research on multicultural education* (3–24). New York: Simon & Schuster/Macmillan.

Banks, T. L. (1995). Two life stories: Reflections of one Black woman law professor. In K. Crenshaw, N. Gotanda, G. Peller, and K. Thomas, eds., *Critical race theory: The key writings that formed the movement* (329–336). New York: New Press.

Bauer, D. and Rhoades, K. (1996). The meanings and metaphors of student resistance. In V. Clark, S. N. Garner, M. Higonnet, and K. H. Katrak, eds., *Anti-feminism in the academy* (95–113). New York: Routledge.

Belenky, M. F., Clinchy, B. M., Goldberger, N.R., and Tarule, J. M. (1986). *Women's ways of knowing: The development of self, voice, and mind.* New York: Basic Books.

Bell, D. (1992). *Faces at the bottom of the well: The permanence of racism.* New York: Basic Books.

Bell-Scott, P., Guy-Sheftall, B., Royster, J. J., Sims-Wood, J., DeCosta-Willis, M., and Fultz, L. P., eds. (1991). *Double stitch: Black women write about mothers and daughters.* New York: HarperPerennial.

Boyd, T. (1995). Put some brothers on the wall! race, representation, and visual empowerment of African American culture. In D. Carson and L. D. Friedman, eds., *Shared differences: Multicultural media and practical pedagogy* (149–164). Urbana, IL: University of Illinois Press.

Boxill, B. R. (1995). Segregation or assimilation? In J. Arthur and A. Shapiro, eds. *Campus wars: Multiculturalism and the politics of difference* (235–248). Boulder, CO: Westview Press.

Breggin, P. R. and Breggin, G.R. (1998). *The war against children of color: Psychiatry targets inner city youth*. Monroe, ME: Common Courage Press.

Butchart, R. E. (1994). Outthinking and outflanking the owners of the world: An historiography of the African-American struggle for education. In M. J. Shujaa, ed. *Too much schooling, too little education: A paradox of Black life in White societies* (85–122). Trenton, NJ: Africa World Press Inc.

Cade, T. (1970). *The Black woman: An anthology*. New York: New American Library.

Carby, H. V. (1985). "On the threshold of woman's era": Lynching, empire, and sexuality in Black feminist theory. *Critical Inquiry* 12: 262–277.

Carlson, D. and Apple, M. W. (1998). Introduction: Critical educational theory in unsettling times. In D. Carlson and M. W. Apple, eds. *Power/knowledge/pedagogy: The meaning of democratic education in unsettling times* (1–38). Boulder, CO: Westview Press.

Carruthers, J. H. (1994). Black intellectuals and the crisis in Black education. In M. J. Shujaa, ed. *Too much schooling, too little education: A paradox of Black life in White societies* (37–55). Trenton, NJ: Africa World Press.

Chapman, A. (1995). *Getting good loving: How Black men and women can make love work*. New York: One World.

Children's Defense Fund (1996). The state of America's children. Washington, D.C.: Children's Defense Fund.

Christian-Smith, L. (1997). Pleasure and danger: Children, media and cultural systems. In S. Muspratt, A. Luke, and P. Freebody, eds. *Constructing critical literacies* (51–58). Cresskill, NJ: Hampton Press.

——— (1999). Strangers in a strange land: A woman studies women's literacies. In L. K. Christian-Smith and K. Kellor, eds. *Everyday knowledge and uncommon truths: Women of the academy* (45–57). Boulder, CO: Westview Press.

Collins, P. H. (1990). *Black feminist thought: Knowledge, conscious-ness, and the politics of empowerment.* New York: Routledge.

Corea, G. (1977). *The hidden malpractice: How American medicine mistreats women.* New York: Jove/HBJ Book.

Crenshaw, K., Gotanda, N., Peller, G., and Thomas, K., eds. (1995). *Critical race theory: The key writings that formed the move-ment.* New York: New Press.

Daniel, J. L. and Allen, A. L. (1988). Newsmagazines, public policy, and the Black agenda. In G. Smitherman and T. A. van Dijk, eds. *Dis-course and discrimination* (23–45). Detroit, MI: Wayne State Uni-versity Press.

Darling-Hammond, L. (1995). Inequality and access to knowledge. In J. A. Banks and C.A.M. Banks, eds. *Handbook of research on multicultural education* (465–483). New York: Simon & Schuster Macmillan.

Darling-Hammond, L. with Green, J. (1994). Teacher quality and equal-ity. In J. I. Goodlad and P. Keating, eds. *Access to knowledge: The continuing agenda for our nation's schools, revised edition.* (237–258). New York: College Entrance Examination Board.

Davis, A. Y. (1981). *Women, race & class.* New York: Vintage Books.

Delpit, L. (1988). The silenced dialogue: Power and pedagogy in educat-ing other people's children. *Harvard Educational Review*, 58(6): 280–298.

Derman-Sparks, L. (1995). How well are we nurturing racial and ethnic diversity? In D. Levine, R. Lowe, B. Peterson, and R. Tenorio, eds. *Rethinking schools: An agenda for change* (17–22). New York: New Press.

Dilks, S. (1998). Response—Dangerous critique: Academic freedom and institutional restraint. In K. Dixon, ed. *Outbursts in academe: Multiculturalism and other sources of conflict* (158–163). Ports-mouth, NH: Boynton/Cook, Heinemann.

Edelsky, C. and Harman, S. (1991). Risks and possibilities of whole lan-guage literacy: Alienation and connection. In C. Edelsky, ed. *With literacy and justice for all: Rethinking the social in language and education* (127–140). London: Falmer Press.

Etter-Lewis, G. (1993). *My soul is my own: Oral narratives of African American women in the professions.* New York: Routledge.

Finders, M. J. (1997). *Just girls: Hidden literacies and life in junior high.* New York: Teachers College Press.

Fox-Genovese, E. (1990). My statue, my self: Autobiographical writings of Afro-American women writers. In H. L. Gates, ed. *Reading Black, reading feminist: A critical anthology* (176–203). New York: Meridian Books.

Franklin, J. H. (1989). *Race and history: Selected essays, 1938–1988.* Baton Rouge, LA: Louisiana State University.

Freydberg, E. H. (1993). American studies: Melting pot or pressure cooker. In J. James and R. Farmer (1993). *Spirit, space and survival: African American women in (White) academe* (49–62). New York: Routledge.

Gay, G. (1993). Building cultural bridges: A bold proposal for teacher education. In F. Schulz, ed. *Annual editions: Multicultural education 95/96* (34–40). Guilford, CT: Dushkin Publishing Group/Brown & Benchmark.

Gersten, R., and Jiminez, R. T. (1994). A delicate balance: Enhancing literature instruction for students of English as a second language. *Reading Teacher,* 47(6), 438–447.

Gilman, S. L. (1985, Autumn). Black bodies, White bodies: Toward an iconography of female sexuality in late nineteenth-century art, medicine, and literature. *Critical Inquiry* 12: 204–242.

Giovanni, N. (1988). *Sacred cows . . . and other edibles.* New York: Quill/William Morrow.

Giroux, H. A. (1990). Reading texts, literacy, and textual authority. *Journal of Education,* 172(1).

Giroux, H. A. and Simon, R. I. (1989). Conclusion: Schooling, popular culture & a pedagogy of possibility. In H.A. Giroux, R. I. Simon, and contributors. *Popular culture, schooling & everyday life* (219–235). Westport, CT: Bergin & Garvey.

Glenn-Paul, D. (1997). Toward a multicultural perspective. In V. Harris, ed. *Teaching multicultural literature in grades K–8* (257–276). Norwood, MA: Christopher-Gordon.

Gordon, B. (1990). The Necessity of African American epistemology for educational theory and practice. *Journal of Education*, 172(3), 88–106.

———— (1994). African-American cultural knowledge and liberatory education: Dilemmas, problems, and potentials in postmodern American society. In M. J. Shujaa, ed. *Too much schooling, too little education: A Paradox of Black life in White societies* (57–78). Trenton, NJ: Africa World Press Inc.

———— (1995). The Fringe dwellers: African American women scholars in the postmodern era. In B. Kanpol and P. McLaren, eds. *Critical multiculturalism: Uncommon voices in a common struggle* (59–88). Westport, CT: Bergin & Garvey.

———— (1995). Knowledge construction, competing critical theories, and education. In J. A. Banks and C.A.M. Banks, eds. *Handbook of research on multicultural education* (184–199). New York: Simon & Schuster Macmillan.

Gore, J. (1998). On the limits to empowerment through critical and feminist pedagogies. In D. Carlson and M. W. Apple, eds. *Power/knowledge/pedagogy: The meaning of democratice education in unsettling times* (271–288). Boulder, CO: Westview Press.

Gould, S. J. (1996). *The mismeasure of man.* New York: W.W. Norton & Company.

Grant, C. A. and Sleeter, C. E. (1994). *Making choices for multicultural education: Five approaches to race, class, and gender.* Englewood Cliffs, NJ: Merrill.

Guinier, L. (1998). *Lift every voice: Turning a civil rights setback into a new vision of social justice.* New York: Simon & Schuster.

Gwaltney, J. L. (1980). *Drylongso: A self-portrait of Black America.* New York: Vintage.

Hansberry, L. (1969). *To be young, gifted, and Black.* New York: Signet.

Hart, A. B. (1906). Slavery and abolition, 1831–1841. New York: Harper and Brothers.

Heath, S. B. (1983). *Ways with words.* New York: Cambridge University Press.

Higginbotham, E. (1982). Two representative issues in contemporary sociological work on Black women. In G. T. Hull, P. B. Scott, and B. Smith, eds. *All the women are White, all the Blacks are men, but some of us are brave: Black women's studies* (93–98). New York: Feminist Press.

hooks, b. (1989). *Talking back: Thinking feminist, thinking Black.* Boston, MA: South End Press.

——— (1990). *Yearning: race, gender, and cultural politics.* Boston, MA: South End Press.

——— (1991). Black women intellectuals. In b. hooks and C. West. *Breaking bread: Insurgent Black intellectual life* (147–164). Boston, MA: South End Press.

——— (1992). Dialectically down with the critical program. In G. Dent, ed. *Black popular culture* (48–55). Seattle, WA: Bay Press

——— (1994). *Outlaw culture: Resisting representations.* New York: Routledge.

——— (1994). *Teaching to transgress: Education as the practice of freedom.* New York: Routledge.

Ideta, L. M. and Cooper, J. M. (1999). Asian women leaders of higher education: Stories of strength and self-discovery. In L. K. Christian-Smith and K. Kellor, eds. *Everyday knowledge and uncommon truths: Women of the academy* (129–146). Boulder, CO: Westview Press.

Irvine, J. J. (1991). *Black students and school failure: Policies, practices and prescriptions.* New York: Praeger Publishers.

James, J. (1993). African philosophy, theory and "living thinkers." In J. James and R. Farmer (1993). *Spirit, space and survival: African American women in (White) academe* (118–135). New York: Routledge.

James, J. and Farmer, R., eds. (1993). *Spirit, space and survival: African American women in (White) academe.* New York: Routledge.

Jewell, K. S. (1993). *From mammy to Miss America and beyond: Cultural images and the shaping of U.S. social policy.* New York: Routledge.

Jipson, J. (1995). Research as autobiography: Imposition/life. In J. Jipson, P. Munro, S. Victor, K. F. Jones, and G. Freed-Rowland, eds. *Repositioning feminism & education: Perspectives on educating for social change* (187–199). Westport, CT: Bergin & Garvey.

Joseph, G. I. (1991). Black mothers and daughters: Traditional and new perspectives. In P. Bell-Scott, B. Guy-Sheftall, J. J. Royster, J. Sims-Wood, M. DeCosta-Willis, and L. P. Fultz, eds. (1991). *Double stitch: Black women write about mothers and daughters* (94–106). New York: HarperPerennial.

Kellor, K. (1999). Her-story: Life history as a strategy of resistance to being constituted woman in academe. In L. K. Christian-Smith and K. Kellor, eds. *Everyday knowledge and uncommon truths: Women of the academy* (25–44). Boulder, CO: Westview Press.

Key, D. (1998). *Literacy shutdown: Stories of six American women.* Newark, DE: International Reading Association and National Reading Conference.

Kimbro, D. and Hill, N. (1991). *Think and grow rich: A Black choice.* New York: Fawcett Columbine.

Kozol, J. (1991). *Savage inequalities: Children in America's schools.* New York: HarperPerennial.

Ladson-Billings, G. (1999). Just what is critical race theory and what's it doing in a nice field like education? In L. Parker, D. Deyhle, and S. Villenas, eds. *Race is . . . race isn't: Critical race theory and qualitative studies in education* (7–30). Boulder, CO: Westview Press.

Lather, P. (1986). Research as praxis. *Harvard Educational Review*, 56(3), 257–273.

Lawrence, C. R. (1995). The word and the river: Pedagogy as scholarship as struggle. In K. Crenshaw, N. Gotanda, G. Peller, and K. Thomas, eds. *Critical race theory: The key writings that formed the movement* (336–351). New York: New Press.

Lewis, M. G. (1993). *Without a word: Teaching beyond women's silence.* New York: Routledge.

——— (1999). The backlash factor: Women, intellectual labour and student evaluation of courses and teaching. In L. K. Christian-Smith and K. Kellor, eds. *Everyday knowledge and uncommon truths: Women of the academy* (59–82). Boulder, CO: Westview Press.

Lorde, A. (1984). *Sister outsider*. Freedom, CA: Crossing Press.

Lipman, M. (1992). Critical thinking: What can it be? In W. Oxman, N. Michelli, and L. Coia (Eds.). *Critical thinking and learning* (55–67). Montclair, NJ: Project Thistle.

Luke, C. (1997). Media literacy and cultural studies. In S. Muspratt, A. Luke, and P. Freebody, eds. *Constructing critical literacies* (19–49). Cresskill, NJ: Hampton Press.

Maher, F. A. and Tetreault, M. K. (1993). Frames of positionality: Constructing meaningful dialogues about gender and race. *Anthropological Quarterly*, 66(3), 118–126.

Mahiri, J. (1998). *Shooting for excellence: African American and youth culture in New Century schools*. Urbana, IL and New York: National Council of Teachers of English and Teachers College Press.

Malveaux, J. (1994). *Sex, lies, and stereotypes: Perspectives of a mad economist*. Los Angeles: Pine One Publishing.

Marable, M. (1996). *Speaking truth to power: Essays on race, resistance, and radicalism*. Boulder, CO: Westview Press.

Marshall, A. (1994). Sensuous Sapphires: A study of the social construction of Black female sexuality. In M. Maynard and J. Purvis, eds. *Researching women's lives from a feminist perspective* (106–124). Bristol, PA: Taylor & Francis.

Maynard, M. (1993). Methods, practice, and epistemology: The debate about feminism and research. In M. Maynard and J. Purvis, eds. *Researching women's lives from a feminist perspective* (10–26). Bristol, PA: Taylor & Francis.

McCall, A. M. (1999). Can feminist voices survive and transform the academy? In L. K. Christian-Smith and K. Kellor, eds. *Everyday knowledge and uncommon truths: Women of the academy* (83–108). Boulder, CO: Westview Press.

McLaren, P. and Gutierrez, K. (1998). Global politics and local antagonisms: Research and practice as dissent and possibility. In D. Carlson and M. W. Apple, eds. *Power/knowledge/pedagogy: The meaning of democratice education in unsettling times* (305–333). Boulder, CO: Westview Press.

Middleton, S. (1993). *Educating feminists: Life histories and pedagogies.* New York: Teachers College Press.

Mitchell, J. (1996). Reflections of a Black social scientist: some struggles, some doubts, some hopes. In T. Beauboeuf-Lafontant and D. S. Augustine, eds. *Facing racism in education, second edition.* Cambridge, MA: Harvard Educational Review (Reprint series no. 28), 69–88.

Mohr, N. (1986). *Going home.* New York: Dial Press.

Morrison, T. (1992). *Playing in the dark: Whiteness and the literary imagination.* New York: Vintage Books.

Morton, P. (1991). *Disfigured images: The historical assault on Afro-American women.* Westport, CT: Praeger Publishers.

Mullings, L. (1997). *On our own terms: Race, class, and gender in the lives of African American women.* New York: Routledge.

National Center for Education Statistics (1993). America's Teachers: Profile of a profession. Washington, D.C.: U.S. Department of Education, Office of Educational Research and Improvement.

Nelson, J. (1993). *Volunteer slavery: My authentic Negro experience.* New York: Penguin Books.

———— (1997). *Straight no chaser: How I became a grown up Black woman.* New York: G.P. Putnam & Sons.

Nieto, S. (1992). We have stories to tell: A case study of Puerto Ricans in children's books. In V. Harris, ed. *Teaching multicultural literature in grades K–8* (173–201). Norwood, MA: Christopher-Gordon.

Noddings, N. (1984). *Caring: A feminine approach to ethics and moral education.* Berkeley, CA: University of California Press.

Olsen, T. (1978). *Silences.* New York: Delacorte Press.

Patterson, O. (1998). *Rituals of blood: Consequences of slavery in two American centuries.* Washington, D.C.: Civitas.

Paul, D. G. (1998). Super-Mammy or Super-Sellout?: Young, Black, and female in academe. In K. Dixon, ed. *Outbursts in academe: Multiculturalism and other sources of conflict* (123–134). Portsmouth, NH: Boynton/Cook, Heinemann.

———— (1999). Images of Black females in Children's/Adolescent contemporary realistic fiction. *Multicultural Review*, 8(2), 34–65.

———— (2000). *Raising Black children who love reading and writing: A guide from birth through grade six.* Westport, CT: Bergin & Garvey.

Postman, N. and Powers, S. (1992). *How to watch TV news.* New York: Penguin Books.

Purves, A. (1993). Toward a reevaluation of reader response and school literature. *Language Arts*, 5, 348–361.

Reyes, M. and Halcon, J. J. (1982). Racism in academia: The Old wolf revisited. In T. Beauboeuf-Lafontant and D. S. Augustine, eds. (1996). *Facing racism in education, second edition.* Cambridge, MA: Harvard Educational Review (Reprint series no. 28), 89–105.

Robbins, J. (1987). *Diet for new America.* New York: Stillpoint Publishing.

Rose, T. (1994). *Black noise: Rap music and Black culture in contemporary America.* Hanover, NH: The University Press of New England.

Ruddick, S. (1980). Maternal thinking. *Feminist Studies*, 6(2), 342–363.

Scully, D. (1980). *Men who control women's health: The mis-education of obstetrician-gynecologists.* Boston: Houghton Mifflin Company.

Shor, I. (1987). *Freire for the classroom: A sourcebook for liberatory teaching.* Portsmouth, NH: Boynton/Cook Publishers.

Siegal, N. (1998). Women in prison: The number of women serving time behind bars has increased dramatically. *Ms. Magazine*, 9(2), 64–72.

Smith, P. (1989). Pedagogy and the popular-culture-commodity-text. In H. A. Giroux, R. I. Simon, and contributors. *Popular culture, schooling and everyday life.* Westport, CT: Bergin & Garvey.

Smitherman, G. (1977). *Talkin and testifyin: The language of Black America.* Detroit, MI: Wayne State University Press.

———— (1988). Discriminatory discourse on Afro-American speech. In G. Smitherman and T. A. van Dijk, eds. *Discourse and discrimination.* Detroit, MI: Wayne State University Press.

Smitherman, G. and van Dijk, T. A., eds. (1988). *Discourse and discrimination.* Detroit, MI: Wayne State University Press.

Steinem, G. (1992). *A revolution from within: A book of self-esteem.* Boston, MA: Little, Brown.

Strickland, D. (1994). Educating African American learners at risk: Finding a better way. *Language Arts,* 71(5), 328–336.

Tannen, D. (1990). *You just don't understand: Women and men in conversation.* New York: Ballantine Books.

Tate, W. F. (1999). Conclusion. In L. Parker, D. Deyhle, and S. Villenas, eds. *Race is . . . race isn't: Critical race theory and qualitative studies in education.* Boulder, CO: Westview.

Trimbur, J. (1989). Consensus and difference in collaborative learning. *College English,* 51(6): 602–616.

Turner, P. A. (1994). *Ceramic uncles & celluloid mammies: Black images and their influence on culture.* New York: Anchor Books.

Vaz, K. (1993). Making room for emancipatory research in psychology: A multicultural feminist perspective. In J. James and R. Farmer, eds. *Spirit, space and survival: African American women in (White) academe* (83–98). New York: Routledge.

Walker, A. (1983). *In search of our mother's gardens: Womanist prose.* San Diego: Harcourt Brace Jovanovich.

Wallace, M. (1998). Variations on negation and the heresy of Black feminist creativity. In H. L. Gates, ed., *Reading Black, Reading Feminist: A critical anthology* (52–67). New York: Meridian Books.

———— (1992). *Boyz in the Hood* and *Jungle Fever.* In G. Dent, ed. *Black popular culture* (123–131). Seattle, WA: Bay Press.

Weiler, K. (1988). *Women teaching for change: Gender, class and power.* Westport, CT: Bergin & Garvey.

White, D. G. (1985). *Arn't I a woman?: Female slaves in the plantation South.* New York: W.W. Norton.

Williams, P. J. (1991). *The alchemy of race and rights: A diary of a law professor.* Cambridge, MA: Harvard University Press.

———— (1996). Talking about race, talking about gender, talking about how we talk. In V. Clark, S. N. Garner, M. Higonnet, and K. H. Katrak, eds. *Anti-feminism in the academy* (69–94). New York: Routledge.

Williams, S. A. (1990). Some implications of Womanist theory. In H. L. Gates, ed. *Reading Black, reading feminist: A critical anthology* (68–75). New York: Meridian Books.

Willis, A. I. (1995). Reading the world of school literacy: Contextualizing the experience of a young African American male. *Harvard Educational Review*, 65(1), 30–49.

Woodson, C. G. (1990). The Mis-education of the Negro. Trenton, NJ: Africa World Press.

Zavella, P. (1996). Feminist insider dilemmas: Constructing ethnic identity with Chicana informants. In D. L. Wolf, ed. *Feminist dilemmas in fieldwork* (138–159). Boulder, CO: Westview Press.

Questions about the Purpose(s) of Colleges and Universities

Norm Denzin,

Josef Progler,

Joe L. Kincheloe,

Shirley R. Steinberg

General Editors

What are the purposes of higher education? When undergraduates "declare their majors," they agree to enter into a world defined by the parameters of a particular academic discourse—a discipline. But who decides those parameters? How do they come about? What are the discussions and proposed outcomes of disciplined inquiry? What should an undergraduate know to be considered educated in a discipline? How does the disciplinary knowledge base inform its pedagogy? Why are there different disciplines? When has a discipline "run its course"? Where do new disciplines come from? Where do old ones go? How does a discipline produce its knowledge? What are the meanings and purposes of disciplinary research and teaching? What are the key questions of disciplined inquiry? What questions are taboo within a discipline? What can the disciplines learn from one another? What might they not want to learn and why?

Once we begin asking these kinds of questions, positionality becomes a key issue. One reason why there aren't many books on the meaning and purpose of higher education is that once such questions are opened for discussion, one's subjectivity becomes an issue with respect to the presumed objective stances of Western higher education. Academics don't have positions because positions are "biased," "subjective," "slanted," and therefore somehow invalid. So the first thing to do is to provide a sense—however broad and general—of what kinds of positionalities will inform the books and chapters on the above questions. Certainly the questions themselves, and any others we might ask, are already suggesting a particular "bent," but as the series takes shape, the authors we engage will no doubt have positions on these questions.

From the stance of interdisciplinary, multidisciplinary, or transdisciplinary practitioners, will the chapters and books we solicit solidify disciplinary discourses, or liquefy them? Depending on who is asked, interdisciplinary inquiry is either a polite collaboration among scholars firmly situated in their own particular discourses, or it is a blurring of the restrictive parameters that define the very notion of disciplinary discourse. So will the series have a stance on the meaning and purpose of interdisciplinary inquiry and teaching? This can possibly be finessed by attracting thinkers from disciplines that are already multidisciplinary, for example, the various kinds of "studies" programs (women's, Islamic, American, cultural, etc.), or the hybrid disciplines like ethnomusicology (musicology, folklore, anthropology). But by including people from these fields (areas? disciplines?) in our series, we are already taking a stand on disciplined inquiry. A question on the comprehensive exam for the Columbia University Ethnomusicology Program was to defend ethnomusicology as a "field" or a "discipline." One's answer determined one's future, at least to the extent that the gatekeepers had a say in such matters. So, in the end, what we are proposing will no doubt involve political struggles.

For additional information about this series or for the submission of manuscripts, please contact Joe L. Kincheloe, 128 Chestnut Street, Lakewood, NJ 08701-5804. To order other books in this series, please contact our Customer Service Department at: (800) 770-LANG (within the U.S.), (212) 647-7706 (outside the U.S.), (212) 647-7707 FAX, or browse online by series at: www.peterlangusa.com.

DATE DUE